The Paisley Thread Industry And The Men Who Created And Developed It

You are holding a reproduction of an original work that is in the public domain in the United States of America, and possibly other countries.You may freely copy and distribute this work as no entity (individual or corporate) has a copyright on the body of the work.This book may contain prior copyright references, and library stamps (as most of these works were scanned from library copies).These have been scanned and retained as part of the historical artifact.

This book may have occasional imperfections such as missing or blurred pages, poor pictures, errant marks, etc. that were either part of the original artifact, or were introduced by the scanning process. We believe this work is culturally important, and despite the imperfections, have elected to bring it back into print as part of our continuing commitment to the preservation of printed works worldwide. We appreciate your understanding of the imperfections in the preservation process, and hope you enjoy this valuable book.

THE PAISLEY THREAD INDUSTRY

Yours very truly,
Matthew Blair

PAISLEY AND ITS INDUSTRIES

MEN WHO CREATED AND

NOTES CONCERNING PAISLEY, ETC.

MATTHEW BLAIR
Author of
"The Paisley Shawl and the Men who Produced it"

ILLUSTRATED

PAISLEY: ALEXANDER GARDNER
Publisher by Appointment to the late Queen Victoria

THE
PAISLEY THREAD
INDUSTRY

AND THE

MEN WHO CREATED AND DEVELOPED IT

WITH

NOTES CONCERNING PAISLEY, OLD AND NEW

BY

MATTHEW BLAIR

Author of
"The Paisley Shawl and the Men who Produced It"

ILLUSTRATED

PAISLEY: ALEXANDER GARDNER
Publisher by Appointment to the late Queen Victoria
1907

PRINTED BY ALEXANDER GARDNER, PAISLEY

TO THOSE

Paisley Men

WHO WERE SCATTERED THE WORLD OVER BY THE
DISASTERS OF THE SHAWL TRADE
BUT WHO EVER RETAINED A WARM AFFECTION
FOR THE SCENES OF THEIR YOUTH

I Dedicate

THIS HISTORY OF THE MARVELLOUS RECOVERY
AND PRESENT PROSPERITY OF THEIR
NATIVE TOWN

PREFACE

IN a previous book the writer attempted to record the history of *The Paisley Shawl, and the Men who Produced It*. That epoch in the life of the town is now closed. It ended in disaster and entailed on Paisley a time of extreme suffering. But to a resolute people, like the descendants of the Paisley weavers, disaster only paves the way for a future success.

Interesting as was the period of the Shawl Trade, it is not more remarkable than the Phœnix-like rise of a new industry, which, in its rapid progress, and gigantic dimensions, is one of the most notable features of the day, and has spread the fame of Paisley to the ends of the earth.

The Thread Trade owes its wonderful success, in a great measure, to the cheap labour thrown upon the market by the collapse of the Shawl Trade; and the present prosperous period, while it has not preserved the old type of workpeople, has developed among the masters and capitalists, qualities quite as remarkable and as honourable to the reputation of the town.

Preface

The present volume is an endeavour to portray the rise of the great Thread Industry for which Paisley has become famous. It is a story of success won by the good old rules of honest work, liberal dealing, and sound business ability; and it is recorded in the hope that this noble example may influence the rising generation of Paisley men.

In the preparation of this work the writer has received assistance from many friends, whose kindness he desires gratefully to acknowledge.

The book cover has been designed by Mrs. Jessie R. Newbery, neé Rowat, a daughter of a family well known in the times of the Paisley Shawl manufacture, and who inherits no small share of the artistic taste of that period.

The Corporation of Paisley, who own the copyright, have kindly granted permission to reproduce Mr. James E. Christie's portrait picture of " The Cross, 1868 "; the presentation portraits of Sir Peter and Mr. Thomas Coats, and the bust of Mr. James Coats, which are preserved in the Art Gallery of the Free Public Library and Museum.

Our veteran townsman, Mr. James Caldwell, F.S.A. (Scot.), Clerk to the County Council of the County of Renfrew; Mr.

James Clark of Chapel House; Mr. Robert Balderston of Ardgowan, Mr. James Hay, and others, have supplied many valuable facts and suggestions. The writer is also indebted to Mr. William Brown, Photographic Artist, for permission to reproduce the historic photograph of "The Last Canal Boat," for his assistance in preparing the illustrations, and for communicating many quaint reminiscences of old times from his abundant store.

THE MOORINGS,
THORNLY PARK, PAISLEY,
December, 1906.

CONTENTS

	PAGE
CHAPTER I.—THE BARGARRAN LINEN THREAD,	17
,, II.—CHANGE TO COTTON, AND CAUSES OF EXPANSION,	24
,, III.—THE CLARK FIRM,	34
,, IV.—THE COATS FIRM,	44
,, V.—OTHER THREAD MANUFACTURERS,	54
,, VI.—COMBINATION,	62
,, VII.—PRESENT POSITION OF THE THREAD INDUSTRY IN PAISLEY,	68
,, VIII.—MANAGEMENT,	79
,, IX.—BENEFACTIONS,	85
,, X.—OLD PAISLEY,	109
,, XI.—TRANSITION,	126
,, XII.—NEW PAISLEY,	182

LIST OF ILLUSTRATIONS

	PAGE
PORTRAIT OF THE AUTHOR,	*Frontispiece*
SPINNING-WHEEL,	18
BARGARRAN HOUSE,	20
BARGARRAN ARMS,	22
HAMMILLS, AND CLARKS' MILLS, 1882,	25
HAMMILLS, AND CLARKS' MILLS, 1906,	26
CLARKS' MILLS, FROM LONEND,	27
FERGUSLIE MILLS,	28
FERGUSLIE MILLS,	29
COATS' MILL IN TORELLÓ, SPAIN,	30
COATS' MILL IN BARCELONA, SPAIN,	31
JAMES CLARK (No. 1), 1747-1829,	35
JAMES CLARK'S HOUSE IN COTTON STREET,	36
JAMES CLARK, 1783-1865,	37
JOHN CLARK, 1791-1864,	37
JAMES CLARK, ESQ., CHAPEL HOUSE,	38
SITE OF CLARK HALLS, 1865, SHOWING WOOD TURNER'S SHOP,	39
CLARK HALLS, FROM CART WALK, 1906,	40
CLARKS' MILLS IN NEWARK, NEW JERSEY, U.S.A.,	41
GEORGE A. CLARK, 1824-1873,	42
WILLIAM CLARK, 1841-1902,	42
STEWART CLARK, ESQ., OF DUNDAS CASTLE,	43
BIRTHPLACE OF JAMES COATS IN CROFT,	45
JAMES COATS, 1774-1857,	46
SIR PETER COATS, 1808-1890,	47
THOMAS COATS, 1809-1883,	48
ANDREW COATS, 1814-1900,	49
COATS' MILL IN PAWTUCKET, RHODE ISLAND, U.S.A.,	50

List of Illustrations

	PAGE
Coats' Mill in St. Petersburg, Russia,	51
Coats' Mill in Pressburg, Hungary,	52
Sir Thomas Glen-Coats, Bart., M.P.,	53
Paisley from the Aqueduct,	55
Carlile Quay,	56
Provost James Carlile, 1752-1835,	57
Alexander Carlile, 1788-1860,	58
Coats' Mills at Ferguslie,	74
Clarks' Mills at Seedhills,	75
Eagley Mills, Bolton,	76
Archibald Coats, Esq.,	77
Half-Timers' School, Ferguslie,	80
Cricket Field, Ferguslie,	81
Girls' Home, Ferguslie,	82
Entrance to Hope Temple Gardens, 1866,	86
Fountain Gardens,	87
Free Public Library and Museum,	88
Shawl Exhibition,	91
Coats Observatory,	93
Artizans' Institution,	95
George A. Clark Town Hall,	97
Coats Memorial Church,	99
Pulpit of Coats Memorial Church,	100
Royal Alexandra Infirmary,	101
Nurses' Home,	103
John Clark of Gateside, 1827-1894,	104
James Clark of Ralston, 1821-1881,	105
Mr. Robert Balderston, Chairman of Infirmary,	106
Gleniffer Home for Incurables,	107
St. Mirren Street, 1865,	111
St. Mirren Street, 1906,	113
Bank of Scotland, Old Causeyside, 1865,	115
Paisley Abbey from Causeyside, 1830,	117
East Side of Causeyside, 1892	118

List of Illustrations

	PAGE
The Charleston Drum,	119
"Peter's," 1901,	120
"Peter's," 1906,	121
Mr. James E. Christie,	123
Paisley Cross, 1868,	124
Key to Paisley Cross, 1868,	125
Cross Steeple and Tollbooth, 1757,	127
Cross Steeple and Saracen's Head Inn, 1868,	128
Cross Steeple, 1870,	129
Cross before Demolitions, 1906,	130
"Hole in the Wa'," 1836,	131
St. Mirren Street, 1906,	132
St. Mirren Street (Water Wynd), 1865,	133
"Diel's Elbow," 1865,	134
Corner of Forbes Street, 1893,	135
Gordon's Loan, 1901,	136
Gordon's Loan, 1906,	137
Corner of Bridge Street, 1865,	138
Corner of Bridge Street, 1906,	139
Causeyside Street, 1892 (Corner of Gordon's Loan),	140
Causeyside Street, 1906,	141
Canal Bank, 1882,	142
Site of Canal Bank, 1906,	143
Robert K. Bell, Provost, 1902-5,	144
Crookston Castle,	145
Carriagehill, 1880,	146
Carriagehill, 1906,	147
Linn at Glenfield,	148
Tannahill Concert,	149
Site of Dunn Square, 1890,	150
Dunn Square, looking West, 1906,	151
Dunn Square, looking East, 1906,	152
Site of George A. Clark Halls, 1865,	154
George A. Clark Halls, 1906,	155

List of Illustrations

	PAGE
Abbey before Restorations, 1835,	156
West Front of Abbey, with Methodist Chapel, 1858,	157
Abbey with Restorations, 1904,	158
The Place of Paisley, 1865,	159
Cross, looking West, 1905,	160
High Street, looking East,	161
"Daunie Weir,"	163
Corner of New Street, 1902,	164
Corner of New Street, 1903,	165
Proposed Building for Young Men's Christian Association,	166
Teetotal Tower, 1860,	167
Birthplace of Professor John Wilson, 1894,	168
Tablet to Professor Wilson, 1906,	169
Hugh Macdonald's "Wee Well,"	170
Stanley Castle,	171
Peesweep Inn,	172
Tannahill's Hole,	173
Tannahill's Birthplace in Castle Street,	174
Tannahill's House, No. 6 Queen Street,	175
The "Coffin En'," 1885,	176
The "Coffin En'," 1905,	177
Mr. William Brown,	179
The Last Canal Boat,	180
David Wilson, Provost, 1900-2,	183
William MacKean, Provost, 1879-82,	187
John Neilson Institution,	189
New Grammar School,	191
Technical College and School of Art,	193
Archibald Mackenzie, Provost, 1894-1900,	195
High Church and Old Grammar School,	197
Mills "Skailing," 1882,	198
Mills "Skailing," 1906,	199
Glasgow Road Promenade, 1906,	201
Arms of Paisley,	202

THE PAISLEY THREAD

CHAPTER I

THE BARGARRAN LINEN THREAD

THE poet tells us there was a time

"When Adam delved and Eve span,"

so that we may conclude that early attempts were made to supersede the proverbial fig leaf.

The making of yarn or thread in Paisley is certainly as old as the weaving of cloth. In early times the two occupations went together. The materials were home-grown wool and flax. The spinning-wheel was in every house, as we learn from many a ballad, and thrifty housewives kept their maids employed in all their spare moments.

Burns, in his "Twa Dugs," says—

"A country girl at her wheel,
Her dizzens done, she's unco weel."

Ladies of even the highest families took pride in their dexterity at the spinning-wheel. The yarn thus spun at home was sent to a "customer weaver," who made it into bed and table-linens. The linen chest, thus amply supplied with the product of fair hands, was drawn upon freely when the young ladies got married.

Many old families still possess, and display with pardonable pride, the wonderfully fine and durable articles made from linen

SPINNING-WHEEL.

yarn spun by their grandmothers. In many cases, also, the spinning-wheel is lovingly preserved, but only now as a drawing-room ornament.

So long as the spinning was done by the hand-wheel, the quality was irregular, and very rough cloth was frequently made from such yarn. The country people brought the produce of their spinning-wheels in to the market along with their eggs and butter, and found a ready sale for it among the weavers of Paisley. Some of the women, however, did produce very fine linen yarn, and this enabled the weavers to make the lawns for which Paisley enjoyed a considerable reputation. In "Lawn Street," such a period is commemorated. Burns, in "Tam o'Shanter," mentions that a certain garment, not remarkable for its longitude was made from "Paisley harn."

But the real founder of the linen yarn for sewing and embroidery purposes was a lady.

Christian Shaw, born about 1685, was a daughter of John Shaw, laird of Bargarran, a small estate near Bishopton, in Erskine Parish, Renfrewshire.

At the age of eleven, this remarkable woman was mixed up with a tragic story of witchcraft. The details, which can be found in *A History of the Renfrewshire Witches* (1877), need not be repeated here. It is sufficient to say that, as a result, seven poor creatures were condemned to the flames for bewitching the girl Christian Shaw. One of them committed suicide in prison, and the remaining six—four women and two men—were actually burned alive, on the Gallow Green of Paisley, on the 10th of June, 1697. This Green was near where Maxwellton Street crosses George Street, and the spot is still marked by a horse shoe inserted in the centre of the causeway. The whole story shows an amount of ignorance, superstition, and cruelty, even among persons of education and position—two hundred and ten years ago—almost beyond belief.

Whatever may have been thought of the part which Christian Shaw played in this tragedy, these facts did not alter her social position, for we find the Bargarran family associating with the best people in the county. In 1718, Christian married the

BARGARRAN HOUSE.

Reverend John Miller, minister of Kilmaurs. Left a widow in 1721, she returned for a time to Bargarran, and afterwards settled in Johnstone.

At that time ladies in good position made a pastime of the spinning-wheel. Mrs. Miller excelled in the production of fine linen yarn, such as was used in Paisley for making lawns, but up till this time it had never been twisted into thread suitable for the sewing or embroidering needle. The idea occurred to her to apply it to these purposes, but no suitable twisting machinery existed in the country. All the thread then in use came from Holland, a country where the textile arts had attained great perfection. Mrs. Miller, through the medium of a friend who was visiting Holland, obtained much valuable information, and also had a twisting mill brought over, which ran twelve bobbins at a time, and was, of course, turned by the hand. With these appliances she succeeded in producing a fine thread, equal or superior to the Dutch, and it is said that she performed every part of the process with her own hands, bleaching the thread on a large slate placed in one of the windows of the house.

The Bargarran family were intimate with their neighbour, Lady Blantyre, who took specimens of the thread to Bath, then a famous resort of the aristocracy. Here it was shown to some makers of lace, for which purpose it was well adapted, and trade immediately resulted. This was in 1722. Mrs. Miller's sisters and the young women of the neighbourhood were instructed in the art, enlarged twining mills were constructed, and a profitable business established.

The Bargarran thread became famous, and, as has happened frequently during the history of the thread trade, the honest producer was imitated by a host of inferior makers, and Bargarran had to fight for its rights. The following advertisement was widely circulated :—

"The Lady Bargarran and her daughters having attained to a great perfection in making, whitening, and twisting of SEWING

THREED, which is as cheap and white, and known by experience to be much stronger than the Dutch, to prevent people's being imposed upon by other threed, which may be sold under the name of 'Bargarran Threed,' the papers in which the Lady Bargarran and her daughters at Bargarran, or Mrs. Miller, her eldest daughter (Christian, now a widow), at Johnstone, do put up their Threed, shall, for direction, have thereupon their Coat

BARGARRAN ARMS.

of Arms, *azure*, three covered cups, *or*. Those who want the said Threed, which is to be sold from fivepence to six shillings per ounce, may write to the Lady Bargarran at Bargarran, or Mrs. Miller at Johnstone, to the care of the Postmaster at Glasgow; and may call for the same in Edinburgh, at John Seaton, merchant, his shop in the Parliament Close, where they will be served either Wholesale or Retail; and will be served in the same manner at Glasgow, by William Selkirk, merchant, in Trongate."

Thus the linen thread manufacture began. Many of the thread makers who took the lead from Mrs. Miller, were quite honourable competitors, and some of them were in Paisley and the neighbouring towns, and there the trade has continued to the present time.

In the *Gentleman's Magazine* for May, 1787, it is stated that, in 1784, there were not less than one hundred and twenty machines at work in twining thread in Paisley, producing 280,000 spindles of thread, the value of which, when finished, amounted to £64,000; and that in the whole of Scotland there were five hundred machines, producing yarn of the value of £220,000; and that this manufacture in Scotland—in performing all the various operations, from the spinning of the flax to the finishing of the thread—employed upwards of twenty thousand women and four or five thousand men. These machines were small, turning only forty-eight bobbins each, and put in operation by manual labour. Cotton has, since those days, largely superseded linen thread, but the latter has its own merits for certain work, and there is still a considerable manufacture of linen thread in Johnstone and district, now made, of course, in all its processes, by the latest improvements in machinery.

The existence in the town of so many hand-twisting mills for linen thread led naturally to the production of cotton thread when the inventions of Arkwright and Crompton placed the fine cotton yarn of Lancashire on the market.

CHAPTER II

CHANGE TO COTTON—CAUSES OF EXPANSION

THE Bargarran thread was linen, a fibre well adapted to sewing thread because of its strength. Its defects were that it was uneven and rough, and could not be spun to a very fine count. Cotton, which possessed better spinning properties, but less strength, became its powerful, and ultimately, successful competitor.

So long as both fibres were spun by the hand spinning-wheel, cotton made no great progress, but, as early as 1738, efforts had been made to improve the methods of spinning. The inventions of Hargreaves, 1764, Arkwright, 1768, and particularly Crompton's "mule" in 1779, entirely revolutionised the cotton industry. Muslins made by the cheap labour of Hindostan had been placed on the British market by the East India Company, at prices against which no European weaver could compete. A demand for a protective duty was pressingly urged towards the close of the eighteenth century, but invention solved the problem in another and better way.

The fine yarn which could now be made so cheaply by Crompton's mule, and the power-loom which speedily followed, completely turned the current of trade. Lancashire was now enabled to produce goods, even with well paid labour, at prices far below those of India, and a trade to the East arose, and these cotton fabrics form now one of our most important exports.

Having access now to a sufficiently fine count of clean and smooth cotton yarn, the Paisley twisters could make a six-cord

HAMMILLS, AND CLARKS' MILLS, 1882.

cable thread, perhaps not quite so strong as linen, but strong enough for all ordinary purposes, much more smooth, and greatly cheaper. King Cotton had gained the day.

Up till the end of the eighteenth century, the cotton imported into this country was chiefly from the West Indies. The new inventions in spinning very much increased the demand, and the planters of the Southern States of North America took up the cultivation with vigour, and soon surpassed all other producers, both for quality and quantity.

The practical monopoly of the United States in the supply of this useful fibre, has led to speculation and many difficulties, and

Hammills, and Clarks' Mills, 1906.

great efforts are now being made to extend the cultivation in other countries. This is the more necessary, as the home consumption of cotton in the United States is very large, and rapidly increasing.

In the specialisation of industries which is constantly taking place, it has happened that Lancashire has some economic advantages for the production of fine cotton yarn. The Paisley thread makers have, therefore, wisely directed their efforts to improvements in the twisting and spooling of the Lancashire yarn. Spinning of fine cotton yarn has only in recent years been

CLARKS' MILLS, FROM LONEND.

attempted by the Coats firm, so that even yet the bulk of the material used comes from Lancashire.

The system of numbering sewing thread was settled at a time when the yarn was all three-cord, and was named according to the count of the single yarn. Thus "30's 3-cord" was made from three strands of 30's single cotton. 30's single cotton means that thirty hanks, each of 840 yards, will weigh one pound. When six-cord thread was introduced, the thread numbers were retained, but a single yarn twice as fine was employed. Thus "30's thread 6-cord" is made from six strands of 60's single cotton. The finished thread remains the same thickness whether three or six-cord, and so suits the same needle. The finest sewing thread

Ferguslie Mills.

now in general use is 100's, made from six strands of No. 200's single cotton. The twist on the single thread is to the left, and that on the plied thread is to the right, which produces the cable character.

At first this thread was sold in hanks, but the wooden spool came into use as soon as the product became a mill or factory made article. Spooling machinery has been greatly improved, and is now practically all automatic.

As every commercial man knows, there are constant alterations taking place in the conditions under which business can be made profitable. The most experienced and estimable of

FERGUSLIE MILLS.

men are not proof against these economic changes. Even when they foresee them, they may have their capital locked up in plant which cannot be utilised, and so no effort can avoid disaster. On the other hand, it often happens that economic changes occur unexpectedly which cause a rush of success and profit for those who happen, possibly from no merit of their own, to be able to take advantage of the position thus created.

"There is a tide in the affairs of men
Which, taken at the flood, leads on to fortune."

The shawl trade may be said to belong to the first of these illustrations—the thread trade to the latter.

Coats' Mill in Torelló, Spain.

The decay of the shawl trade was not due to any deficiency or fault of the manufacturers. The fashion changed, and the demand ceased. Fashion is not regulated by the rules of political economy. We would naturally expect that the more convenient and suitable for its purpose an article can be made, and the cheaper it can be put on the market, the larger would be the demand. But such rules do not apply to an object of fashion, as, for instance, a lady's bonnet. It must be in the fashion, or it is of no use at all. Fashion may decree that it must be of a shape that violates all the conditions of convenience which a covering for the head should possess, yet the article must be of that form, no matter what torment the wearer may

COATS' MILL IN BARCELONA, SPAIN.

suffer. The discomfort is gladly borne, and the price is wholly disregarded.

That an article so useful, graceful, and beautiful as the Paisley shawl should be in a few years totally neglected, was a thing hardly to be believed. But so it was. The demand ceased, and no energy or ability of the manufacturers could revive it.

Shakespeare says that—

" Some are born great, some achieve greatness,
And some have greatness thrust upon them."

The gift of cheap labour was thrust upon the thread manufacturers. They did nothing to produce this state of affairs, and, indeed, no doubt regretted it, but they had the wisdom to make the most of the position, to the great advantage of all concerned.

One of the controlling causes, therefore, which made the business settle in Paisley in preference to other places, was the cheap labour thrown upon the market by the decay of the shawl trade. About the same time there occurred the invention of the sewing machine, which created an increased demand for thread. In this case, again, the thread manufacturers had prosperity unexpectedly placed within their reach. They did not invent the sewing machine—they were only in an excellent position to take advantage of it.

As usual, a machine of this kind is an evolution. Many attempts at sewing machines had been made, but the first that was really successful was brought out, in 1846, by Elias Howe, an American. The Wheeler & Wilson, the Singer, and many other Manufacturing Companies, followed with variations and improvements adapted to different trades.

Like every other labour-saving invention, the sewing machine displaced labour, and at first caused much suffering. This was inevitable; but in the end, as always happens, the change materially improved the conditions of existence. The invention brought about an enormous extension of business, many articles of clothing were now placed within the reach of the humblest classes, and many comforts and conveniences arose from the introduction of this machine. It created an enlarged demand for thread. The Paisley firms had a good name and a hold upon the market, and their business expanded rapidly with the demand. Their success provoked competition, which compelled them to keep their methods of production abreast of the latest improvements, and this has always been a characteristic of the leading Paisley firms.

But however they may have deserved success by their business ability, they are much indebted to the decay of the shawl trade and the invention of the sewing machine. These factors created the position, which the thread manufacturers have, with consummate ability, utilized to evolve the present immense business.

CHAPTER III

THE CLARK FIRM

THE history of the cotton spool trade in Paisley is inseparably connected with the family of Clark. They were engaged in it from the commencement, and amidst all the changes that have taken place, the firm of Clark & Co. has maintained its prominent place.

The story is interesting, and well worthy of being put on record. In 1753, William Clark, a farmer at Dykebar, near Paisley, died, leaving a widow and six young children, none of them old enough to continue the farm. The family, therefore, moved into the town of Paisley to obtain employment. Their means were slender, but they had a fair stock of that grit which distinguishes the Scottish peasantry, and which is the most valuable asset of our nation. Inured to labour and accustomed to thrift, "poortith," as Burns calls it, has no terrors for this class of people. It only acts as a stimulant. They soon learned to laugh at calamity, and out of disaster to carve a victory, and so the Clark family, by dint of hard work and careful habits, got on well in the world.

At that time weaving was prosperous in Paisley. The work was light and well paid. The weavers usually ceased their labours in the afternoon, and, attired in their best, went out for a promenade and a crack. There was, therefore, at this time a steady stream of incomers, which were entirely Scotch, the unskilled labour being from the Highlands. The Irish element did not make a pronounced appearance in Paisley till the time of the Famine, in 1846. The study of such directories

JAMES CLARK (No. 1), 1747-1829.

as exist, shows that many of the families now numerous in Paisley came into the town at this period, and among them the family of the Clarks, which had hardly any representatives in the town before that date.

James Clark, No. 1 (1747-1829), one of the sons of William Clark, commenced the business of weavers' furnisher and heddle twine manufacturer in Cotton Street, and it may be mentioned in passing, that he had at one time in his employment Alexander

Wilson, afterwards the famous American ornithologist, and author of "Watty and Meg." Thread or cord for heddles and harness was in good demand. This was made on the hand-twisting frame similar to that introduced from Holland for the Bargarran thread, and was usually turned by a stout Highlander. There were many

JAMES CLARK'S HOUSE IN COTTON STREET.

of these small firms of twisters in Paisley in those days, and the material they used was principally linen.

The loop or eye of the heddle was made of fine silk, as that part required to be particularly smooth. The silk was, of course, imported. On 20th November, 1806, Napoleon issued his famous Berlin Decree, by which an interdict was placed on the commerce of Britain, and the supply of silk ceased. In this predicament James Clark's brother, Patrick, turned his attention to perfecting in smoothness a cotton thread, and, as the inventions of Hargreaves, Arkwright, and Crompton had now placed fine cotton yarn on the market, he succeeded in producing a smooth cotton heddle yarn which replaced the silk. This improvement continued till cotton for heddles entirely superseded silk. Thus it may be remarked that Napoleon and the Clark family between them,

JAMES CLARK, 1783-1865.   JOHN CLARK, 1791-1864.
FIRM OF J. & J. CLARK.

have the credit of introducing the making of fine cotton thread into Paisley.

The year 1812 may be taken as the earliest date upon which Clark's sewing thread was placed upon the market.

Two of the sons of James Clark, No. 1, James (1783–1865), and John (1791–1864), formed the firm of J. & J. Clark, and erected a factory in Seedhills. Hand machines had by this time been discarded, and the thread trade had become a factory industry.

The James Clark of Messrs. J. & J. Clark was the first to introduce spool cotton sewing thread. We are indebted to his son, Mr. James Clark, of Chapel House, for an explanation of the circumstances of this very important and interesting development. Mr. Clark says :—

JAMES CLARK, ESQ., CHAPEL HOUSE.

"Originally the cotton thread was sold in hanks or skeins, and then ladies had to wind it into little balls, as they generally wind a cut of wool yarn at the present day. Wishing to convenience his fair customers, James would, on selling a skein of cotton thread, sit down at a weaver's pirn wheel, and wind the thread upon a spool, for which he charged a half-penny, but that half-penny he refunded when the empty spool was returned to him.

The spools cost sixpence a dozen, and were ordered by James, to the extent of half a gross at a time, from a wood turner named Robert Paul, which he carried home in his coat pocket, to wind thread thereon by his own hand, if desired, after the sale of a skein had been effected by him."

Site of Clark Halls, 1865, showing Wood Turner's Shop.

The turner's shop stood on the site which is now covered by the Clark Town Hall.

Since these days, spooling machinery has been marvellously perfected, and is now practically automatic, winding and measuring the thread with extreme accuracy and neatness.

The mills at Seedhills continued to prosper and increase, and the third, and even the fourth, generation of the Clark family have managed them with hereditary ability. They worked more for the home than for the foreign markets, but they had an important trade with America. When the United States entered upon a policy of high protection, the Clark firm erected extensive

CLARK HALLS, FROM CART WALK, 1906.

mills in Newark in New Jersey. This department was under the care of Mr. George A. Clark (1824–1873), and afterwards of Mr. William Clark (1841–1902), sons of John Clark.

The success of Clark's thread was due to the fact that it was always a sound article, and of a guaranteed length. As usual, this produced a host of imitators. Not only was the name unblushingly copied, but the trade mark of an anchor was imitated in ingenious ways. All makers of honest thread, and there are many such in Scotland, England, and America, have had to suffer in this way. But all these interlopers sooner or later came to grief, and Clarks' "Anchor" thread survived and maintained its reputation.

CLARKS' MILLS IN NEWARK, NEW JERSEY, U.S.A.

The competition between the several thread makers in Paisley, and notably between the firms of Clark and Coats, was at times very severe, but between these two firms it was always honourable and without bitterness. Each strove to supply the wants of the public, and they pushed their independent lines of business, preserving their clear individuality. The way was thus prepared for that great amalgamation which has resulted in important economies in administration and distribution. The public has been well served, and the enterprising thread makers have reaped the reward. Nor have they been remiss in showing, by their benefactions to the town, that they fully appreciate the responsibilities as well as the privileges of success. The firm was

GEORGE A. CLARK, 1824-1873.   WILLIAM CLARK, 1841-1902.

formed into a limited liability company in 1896, under the name of Clark & Company, Limited, and the amalgamation with J. & P. Coats, Limited, took place on 6th August, 1896.

Several members of the Clark family have occupied public positions in the town, and all of them have been unwearied in their work on philanthropic and religious societies and associations

Mr. James Clark of Ralston was a member of the Town Council, and Bailie in 1859.

Mr. James Clark of Chapel House was Provost of Paisley from 1882 to 1885.

Mr. Stewart Clark, now of Dundas Castle, represented the Burgh in Parliament from 1884 to 1885.

STEWART CLARK, ESQ., OF DUNDAS CASTLE.

CHAPTER IV

THE COATS FIRM

THE founder of this business was James Coats (1774-1857). He came of several generations of Paisley weavers, than which no better ancestry need be desired by any man, and he exhibited in his life many of the best characteristics of these remarkable men. He even had his share of the poetical faculty, though dormant, for he was the intimate friend and companion of Robert Tannahill and R. A. Smith. Integrity and enterprise were the leading traits in his character, and have been conspicuous among all his descendants, who, when fortune favoured them, developed a large and free-handed liberality.

After serving his apprenticeship to the weaving, Mr. Coats enlisted in the Ayrshire Fencibles, a cavalry regiment, and spent six years in the army. This time was not lost. The habits of order, obedience, and reliability, fostered by military training, proved of great advantage in after life. Advocates of a compulsory short term of service in the army for all our young men, will find much in the career of James Coats to support their views.

On leaving the army, in 1796, he resumed the weaving. He married in 1802, and shortly thereafter began manufacturing on his own account. He was shrewd enough to observe and follow the changes in fashion which are the great risks of a fancy trade. On one of his visits to London he bought a Canton crape shawl, intending it as a present for his wife. At that time all the beautiful specimens of crape weave came from China. No attempt had been made, at least in Scotland, to

BIRTHPLACE OF JAMES COATS, IN CROFT.

manufacture this article, which required special skill and knowledge. The material was silk. Silk manufacture had been introduced into Paisley by Humphrey Fulton, in 1760, so that the material and the skilled labour were at hand. Mr. Coats had made several attempts to produce crape, when he discovered that another manufacturer, Mr. James Whyte, had been engaged on the same endeavour with no better success. They agreed to combine their knowledge, entered into partnership, and, in the end, succeeded; and for some years had practically a monopoly of the Canton crape trade. This was a profitable enterprise, and laid the foundations of Mr. Coats' fortune. He built a house in Back Row, Ferguslie, and was now a person of means, but he was a far-seeing man, and well aware of the uncertainties attending the manufacture of an article of fashion. It was when

JAMES COATS, 1774-1857.
From Bust in Museum.

engaged in the Canton crape trade that he first conceived the idea of founding a manufactory of sewing thread.

One important element in the crape production is the peculiar twist required for the yarn. This process Mr. Coats had done for him by Messrs. Ross & Duncan, a firm of twisters engaged in the thread trade, who had a small factory at 66 George Street. This firm requiring more capital, Mr. Coats entered as a sleeping partner, and thus had an opportunity of acquiring a complete knowledge of the business. The trade increased, and

Sir Peter Coats, 1808-1890.
From presentation portrait in Art Gallery of Free Public Library and Museum, painted, in 1881, by Sir Daniel Macnee, P.R.S.A.

on expiry of the contract, in 1826, Messrs. Ross & Duncan erected a factory in another part of the town, and Mr. Coats built a small mill at Ferguslie, where he started thread making with an engine of twelve horse power. This building has been incorporated with, and still forms part of, the vast works at Ferguslie.

Thomas Coats, 1809-1883.
From presentation portrait in Art Gallery of Free Public Library and Museum, painted, in 1881, by Sir Daniel Macnee, P.R.S.A.

Mr. Coats retired from active business in 1830, giving over the manufacturing department to his partners and his son William, and placing the thread business in the hands of his sons James (1803-1845) and Peter (1808-1890), under the firm of J. & P. Coats. Shortly afterwards, another son, Thomas (1809-1883), was admitted a partner. The combination was excellent, and shows the forethought and care of the father in training his sons. James was a manufacturer, Peter had received

Andrew Coats, 1814-1900.

a mercantile education in Glasgow, and Thomas had been trained as an engineer.

From that time, the firm of J. & P. Coats went steadily and successfully forward, constantly extending, and supplying the home and foreign markets. In 1840, three-fourths of their trade was with America. A younger brother, Andrew Coats (1814-1900), was sent out to manage the selling department of the business in the United States, and continued to do so for twenty years with marked prudence and ability.

Various changes occurred in the firm from time to time. Mr. James Coats died unmarried in 1845, but several of the sons of Mr. Peter (who received the honour of knighthood in 1869) and of Mr. Thomas became partners; taking the burden

COATS' MILL IN PAWTUCKET, RHODE ISLAND, U.S.A.

off their fathers' shoulders and displaying the same admirable business qualities as their parents.

The popularity of Coats' thread was due to its invariably excellent and uniform quality and guaranteed length, but, as usual, a host of counterfeits sprang up. The audacity and immorality of some of these imitations surpass belief. Thread of inferior quality was unblushingly labelled with Coats' name, and spools purporting to contain three hundred yards frequently had not more than a hundred and fifty yards. Not till the law had been invoked and severe penalties inflicted, were these practices arrested. But the law courts in all countries

COATS' MILL IN ST. PETERSBURG, RUSSIA.

have invariably supported the Coats' case, and one by one, at great trouble and expense, these interlopers were ultimately exposed and interdicted.

When a policy of high protection was adopted by the United States, Messrs. Coats erected mills at Pawtucket, in Rhode Island State—between 1870 and 1883—under the management of the eldest son of Sir Peter Coats, now Sir James Coats, Bart., of Auchendrane, Ayrshire; and these mills have now grown to be as large as those at Paisley.

But the Paisley production never slackened. New markets were found, and, in cases where high duties stood in the way,

COATS' MILL IN PRESSBURG, HUNGARY.

mills were erected abroad. Thus considerable establishments have in recent times been opened in Russia, Germany, Austria, Hungary, and Spain.

A further step forward was taken in 1890, when the business was transformed into a Limited Liability Company, with a capital of £5,750,000, and the prospectus states that the average annual profits for the previous seven years had been £426,048 13s. 9d.

Two-thirds of the shares and stock were issued to the public, the customers of the firm and employees receiving due consideration. The prosperity of the company has since been marvellous, and those investors who retained their shares found, in a few years,

SIR THOMAS GLEN-COATS, BART., M.P. FOR WEST RENFREWSHIRE.

that their investment had multiplied many times, as referred to at greater length in another chapter.

The Coats family have not, as a rule, desired political position, but Sir Thomas Glen-Coats, Bart., of Ferguslie Park, is presently M.P. for West Renfrewshire.

CHAPTER V

OTHER THREAD MANUFACTURERS

BESIDES the firms of Clark and Coats, there were many other thread manufacturers who gained considerable reputation in their day. In most cases, however, they succumbed in the end to the inevitable economic rule, that any business which is keenly competed cannot be carried on profitably except on a large scale. Those who could not extend sufficiently, one by one dropped out of the race, or were absorbed by the larger firms. Some of them, no doubt, were simply counterfeiters, but others were quite honourable competitors.

The Directories of Paisley which are preserved in the Free Library begin at 1784. There is then a blank till 1812, and a further blank between 1814 and 1820, after which date only an occasional volume is awanting. From these imperfect materials we gather some interesting details, but the reader must remember that we only state such facts as are found in the existing Directories.

The total number of so-called thread manufacturers is one hundred and seven, but of these more than half only appear for one or two years, and probably were not really manufacturers at all. Some businesses have evidently been carried on by the same family for two or three generations, with only a slight change in the name of the firm. In other cases, firms of the same name have apparently been created so as to keep separate certain classes of products, or to provide an opening for a time for some of the younger branches of the family. In other cases

PAISLEY FROM THE AQUEDUCT.

amalgamation or absorption has taken place, while the original name of the firm has still been retained in the Directory. Some few are manifestly mere imitators, seeking to benefit by the labours of more able men. There are twenty-three firms of thread manufacturers given in the Directory for 1784, and only three in that of 1906-7—and even these three are now in reality combined into one.

The family which has been longest connected with the thread trade is that of Clark, dating (as far as the Directories state) from 1784 to 1906-7, a period of a hundred and twenty-three years. But, as the first James Clark was born in 1747, he would be thirty-seven years of age in 1784, and so it is possible

Carlile Quay.

that his business as a maker of thread and heddle twine was commenced before that date.

According to the Directories, the family of Carlile has carried on thread manufacture, under firms slightly differing in name, from 1784 till 1886, a period of one hundred and two years. It is possible, in this case also, that the business was in existence before 1784; and, indeed, it has been stated that it was commenced in 1752.

The Carliles have had a long and honourable connection with the industries of the town, and not a few members of that family have been distinguished for public services and literary culture. The first of whom we have any record is John Carlile,

Provost James Carlile, 1752-1835.

born in 1703, who came from Annan, and settled in Paisley in 1742. His son, William, appears in the Directory of 1784 as a thread manufacturer, although he may have begun business before that date. He was the author of an interesting article entitled "New Description of Paisley," which appeared in the *Gentleman's Magazine*, in May, 1787, which contains numerous details regarding the weaving and other industries in Paisley at that time, and from which we extract the facts given at page 23. His son, William Carlile (1746-1829), was a prominent man in his day, and entertained liberal opinions which brought him into some notice during the Radical troubles. He was Provost of Paisley for two terms—1816 to 1818, and 1820 to 1822. His brother, James Carlile (1752-1835), was

ALEXANDER CARLILE, 1788-1860.

Provost of Paisley from 1822 till 1824. Alexander Carlile (1788-1860), a son of James Carlile, was a member of the Town Council, and distinguished for his literary tastes. He was one of the founders of the *Paisley Magazine* in 1828, of which Motherwell the poet was the editor, and he contributed several articles to that publication. He also appears among the *Paisley Poets* as the author, among other poems, of the charming song, "Wha's at the Window, Wha, Wha?" The firm, after an existence of at least a hundred and two years, was absorbed by Messrs. J. & P. Coats in 1887.

Robert Farquharson, thread manufacturer, was Provost in 1824-7, during a time of exceedingly depressed trade, when as many as fifteen thousand persons were wholly or partially dependent on the Relief Funds raised in all parts of the country. He exerted himself greatly to alleviate the suffering, and for this he was ever afterwards held in high esteem by the working people, however much, in later times, he differed from them in political matters.

The firm of Peter Kerr & Son existed from 1812 till 1906, a period of ninety-four years, but this firm did not exclusively make sewing cotton thread.

Messrs. Coats commenced in 1827, so they have had a continuous existence of eighty years.

We give the names and dates of the various firms, but omitting those which appear to have existed less than five years :—

LIST OF THREAD MANUFACTURERS IN PAISLEY DIRECTORIES.

	Year first mentioned.	Year last mentioned.
Carlile, William,	1784	1814
Clark, James,	1784	1833
Carlile, James,	1812	1852
Clark, Matthew,	1812	1823
Clark, Peter,	1812	1820

LIST OF THREAD MANUFACTURERS—*continued.*

	Year first mentioned.	Year last mentioned.
Carswell, Robert,	1812	1835
Davidson, John,	1812	1820
Ferguson, John,	1812	1835
Kerr, Peter, & Son,	1812	1906
Macfarlane, John,	1812	1820
Pattison, Robert,	1812	1823
Stow, William,	1812	1820
Wilkinson, D.,	1812	1820
Wilson, James,	1814	1833
Clark, J. & J., & Compy.,	1820	1905
Halden, Alexander,	1820	1828
Nairn, Thomas,	1820	1832
Young, George,	1820	1830
Carlile, Alexander,	1823	1832
Carlile, Warrand,	1823	1833
Kerr, John, & Sons,	1823	1863
Coats, James,	1827	1831
Morris, John,	1827	1833
Murdoch, William,	1827	1832
Ross & Duncan,	1827	1896
Stirrat, James,	1827	1852
M'Nicol, David,	1828	1835
Carswell, A. & G., & Co.,	1830	1835
Coats, J. & P.,	1832	1906-1907
Jack, Robert,	1832	1859
Glen, Anderson, & Co.,	1833	1849

LIST OF THREAD MANUFACTURERS—*continued.*

	Year first mentioned.	Year last mentioned.
Kerr, Thomas,	1833	1845
Clapperton & Co.,	1835	1886
Farquharson, Robert,	1837	1860
Roger, Manson & Co.,	1845	1860
Anderson, James,	1849	1890
Kerr & Clark,	1852	1882
Coats, J. & T.,	1854	1860
Carlile, James, & Sons,	1859	1886
Clark, J. & R.,	1859	1866
Clark & Co.,	1862	1906-1907
Clark, James, & Co.,	1862	1884
Clark, J. & Co.,	1865	1881
Kerr & Co.,	1873	1906-1907
Glenfield Thread Company,	1876	1881

Many of the leading men in these smaller firms were gentlemen of high culture and public spirit, and of great usefulness to the community in their day, although not privileged to leave behind them any stately memorials. As with many of the humbler ingenious workmen, they contributed their share to the building up of the great industry for which the town is now celebrated. They may have anticipated the success, but did not survive to share in it. In every warfare there are many brave men who only find a place among the unrecorded dead.

CHAPTER VI

COMBINATION

IN dealing with an article of general consumption, which, like sewing thread, is supplied to the public by shopkeepers, the manufacturer finds that the costs of distribution are very great. His customers are counted by many thousands, and to keep up the amount of sales and compete with rivals, a large staff of travellers must be continually on the road. The cost of advertising has also to be considered, and this is often enormous. These expenses of distribution must, with some well-known articles, be more than the whole original cost of the product.

Even the largest firms cannot afford to despise economies in distribution, and in the Thread trade this naturally suggested some form of co-operation between the various makers.

In 1889, Messrs. Clark and Coats formed a distributing combination under the name of "The Sewing Cotton Agency," which was shortly afterwards altered to "The Central Agency," when an additional firm—Messrs. Jonas Brook & Brothers of Meltham—joined it.

· The business of the Agency was to maintain the travellers, regulate the sales, and collect the accounts, thus greatly reducing the staffs which had previously been necessary. The individuality of each firm in all else but distribution was not affected. The work of the Agency was controlled by delegates from the firms interested, the expenses were apportioned among them, and an important economy was the result.

The success of these arrangements suggested a more organic union. This important step was taken on 1st July, 1896, when the business of Messrs. Coats, which, as already mentioned, had been converted in 1890 into a Limited Liability Company, was amalgamated with those of Messrs. Clark & Company of Paisley, Messrs. Jonas Brook & Brothers of Meltham, and Messrs. James Chadwick & Brother of Bolton. For this purpose the capital of J. & P. Coats, Limited, was readjusted, new shares created and issued to the other Companies, and additional directors appointed. Each of the other Companies, however, maintains a separate existence, the names and trade marks are preserved and used where these are associated with particular markets or qualities of thread, but the whole profits are distributed among the shareholders of J. & P. Coats, Limited, the capital of which now amounts to nearly £11,000,000, and the shareholders number about 17,000.

The Selling Department is conducted under the name of "The Central Agency, Limited," as taking the place of the former "Central Agency," and the Agency also undertakes the sale of the sewing silk threads of Messrs. Lister & Company of Bradford, and has recently been entrusted with the distribution work of the English Sewing Cotton Company, Limited, much to the advantage of all concerned.

Much has been said of the "practical" monopoly created by the combination of these firms, but such charges are wholly without foundation. A monopoly cannot exist in a free market. So long as the market is free, a successful manufacturer may secure a large part or nearly all of the trade, but there is no monopoly. He obtains his trade solely because he gives the best value to the consumer. This is the whole secret of the so-called Coats monopoly. No restrictive legislation has created it. No "log rolling" has been employed to reach the present position. It is perfectly fair and legal. Objectors are free to compete if they choose. And they do so. The chairman of the Company stated, in 1897, that there were more than twenty sewing cotton manufacturers in this country, and some of them large and wealthy, and over forty on the Continent of Europe, all competing with Messrs. Coats in a free market. This statement is now much within the mark, for at present there are about forty home firms, of more or less importance, making sewing cotton in competition with J. & P. Coats, Limited, apart altogether from any of the firms included in the English Sewing Cotton Company, Limited. There are also several wholesale houses who have factories for winding and twisting sewing cotton. A reliable authority has stated that there are at least 180 firms outside the Coats combination freely supplying the same markets.

The business of Messrs. Coats has been built up by careful study of the wants and interests of the consumers. Buyers have learned the superiority of Coats' and Clarks' thread, and insist on having it, and a reputation thus attained is not easily disturbed. It is a monopoly of capacity. These firms are only reaping the well-deserved harvest following upon years of laborious effort.

Nor can it be said with truth that the interests of the consumers of sewing thread have been neglected, in order to make exceptionally large profits. The price obtained is the normal competition value in a perfectly free market, and is fixed by causes which the Messrs. Coats did not create, and from the operation of which, whether for their benefit or against it, they cannot escape.

A manufacturer has to deal with two markets, neither of which he can control. Messrs. Coats cannot buy their raw cotton, spun yarn, or labour at a less price than is given for these factors of production by other competitors. They must pay the market price, or go without the article. In like manner, they cannot sell their product for more than the public will give for it, or for a higher price than other makers are offering to take for an equal article. Such is the unalterable economic position of all manufacturers. The price they can buy and sell at is not of their fixing, and is beyond their grasp.

But between these two markets lies the region where profit can be made. The manufacturer who, by skill and economy can diminish the amount spent on production and distribution receives, and rightly receives, the reward of his ability, as, in the contrary case, he would receive the punishment of his incapacity. This is the sphere in which the Coats combination make their large profits. They deal in sums so large, that a small percentage of waste, extravagance, or incapacity in management, would amount in a year to a fabulous sum. On the other hand, wise economies and good organization in production and distribution secure profits which are large because the business is large. Messrs. Coats' accounts comprise the profits of sixteen separate and distinct manufacturing concerns, the returns from over sixty branch houses, and, in addition they have more than a hundred and fifty depots in all parts of the world, and they have over seven thousand different prices, and sell in thirty foreign currencies. Their ledger accounts exceed a hundred thousand.

Further, it may be said that the Protective legislation of some foreign countries, not intended to benefit us, has done not a little to swell the profits of Messrs. Coats' shareholders. The chairman of the Company, in 1899, stated that they held shares in twelve manufacturing concerns in foreign countries, and by far the larger part of their entire profits was derived from investments in these companies, and not from mills in the United Kingdom. The explanation is simple. The selling price in these Protective countries is maintained by the tariff at a high level expressly to benefit the local producer. This, in many cases, makes him easy about improving his methods. When, therefore, there comes upon the scene a manufacturer so thoroughly versed by long experience in all the economies of production as are the Messrs. Coats (the selling price being still kept up by the tariff), a very substantial margin of profit falls to his share. No doubt the foreign statesmen who enacted these tariffs did not intend to favour British enterprise at the expense of their own people, but that is the result which their action has produced; and this is not the only case in which hostile foreign tariffs have worked out so as to compel the foreigner to pay tribute to this country.

The great combination grew naturally out of economic conditions, and far from being an injury to the community, it is a great benefit, and is in itself a most interesting object lesson, as showing in a very marked manner the success which always follows the application of integrity, enterprise, and perfect organization.

CHAPTER VII

PRESENT POSITION OF THE THREAD INDUSTRY IN PAISLEY

THE present position of the thread industry in Paisley can best be placed before our readers by reproducing the most recent Report and Balance Sheet of Messrs. J. & P. Coats, Limited, for the year ending 30th June, 1906.

To this Report we may add an estimate of the present market value (buyers) of the different forms of the Capital:—

CAPITAL OF J. & P. COATS, LIMITED.	FACE VALUE.	Stock Exchange List, 1st December, 1906 (Buyers).	SALEABLE VALUE.
Preference Shares (£10 each),	£2,500,000	£16⅜	£4,093,750
Preferred Ordinary Stock (£10 each),	3,000,000	£49½	14,850,000
Ordinary Shares (£1 each),	4,500,000	£6 5s. 3d.	28,181,250
Debenture Stock (£100 each),	917,420	£109	999,987
	£10,917,420		£48,124,987

Even those who have little aptitude for understanding figures, will readily observe from this statement that a property which the shareholders purchased for eleven millions sterling, has become so valuable and popular that there are buyers in the market willing to pay forty-eight millions for it.

J. & P. COATS, LIMITED.

DIRECTORS.

ARCHIBALD COATS, *Chairman*.
SIR JAMES COATS, BART.
SIR THOMAS GLEN-COATS, BART., M.P.
SIR JAMES KING, BART.
SIR WILLIAM ARROL.
CHARLES LEWIS BROOK.
STEWART CLARK.
KENNETH M. CLARK.
J. O. M. CLARK.
PETER COATS.

GEORGE COATS.
PETER MACKENZIE COATS.
WILLIAM HODGE COATS.
P. HERBERT COATS.
ERNEST S. COATS.
T. J. HIRST.
O. E. PHILIPPI.
E. A. PHILIPPI.
W. P. STEWART.

Secretary, W. P. STEWART.   *Asst. Secy.*, CHARLES MONEY.

REPORT OF THE DIRECTORS

TO BE SUBMITTED TO THE SIXTEENTH ANNUAL ORDINARY GENERAL MEETING, TO BE HELD IN THE MERCHANTS' HALL, 1 WEST GEORGE STREET, GLASGOW, ON THURSDAY, THE 29th DAY OF NOVEMBER, *1906*, AT TWELVE O'CLOCK NOON.

The Directors beg to submit to the Shareholders the Report and Statement of Accounts for the year to 30th June, 1906.

The Net Profit for the year, after carrying the sum of £41,797 11s. 9d. to Depreciation Account, amounts to £2,974,088 9s. 4d. (including £63,933 3s. 5d., which properly belongs to last year). This, with £479,908 8s. 8d. brought forward from last year, makes a total of £3,453,996 18 0
and after deducting Debenture Interest, paid and accrued for the year, Dividend of 6 per cent. on Preference Shares, Quarterly Dividends on Preferred Ordinary Stock and Ordinary Shares, paid to 30th June, and Income Tax, etc., as per Balance Sheet, ... 1,409,284 12 9

£2,044,712 5 3

and final Quarterly Dividends for the year ended 30th June, paid since that date on—
Preferred Ordinary Stock, 30th September, 5 per cent. ; ... £150,000 0 0
Ordinary Shares, 30th September, 5 per cent., ... 225,000 0 0

375,000 0 0

there remains a balance of £1,669,712 5 3
which the Directors recommend should be dealt with as follows :—
To Dividend Reserve Fund Account, ... £450,000 0 0
„ Bonus of 1s. per Share, ... 225,000 0 0
„ Pension Fund Account, ... 120,100 19 9
„ Marine and Fire Underwriting Account, ... 149,528 4 9
„ Debenture Premium Account, ... 25,000 0 0

969,629 4 6

leaving a balance to be carried forward of £700,083 0 9
which is subject to Auditors' Fees, Bonus, etc.

In terms of the Articles of Association and the order of retirement arranged, the following Directors, Sir THOMAS GLEN-COATS, Bart., M.P., Sir WILLIAM ARROL, Messrs. PETER COATS, P. M. COATS, W. H. COATS, and E. S. COATS, retire at this time, and are eligible for re-election. The Board recommends their re-election.

The Directors beg to report that, having considered it advisable during the year to add another Director to the Board, they elected Mr. E. ALEX. PHILIPPI a Director of the Company, and now recommend the Shareholders to confirm his election.

The Auditors, Messrs. TURQUAND, YOUNGS & CO., and Mr. DAVID W. KIDSTON, being eligible, offer themselves for re-election.

BY ORDER OF THE BOARD,

W. P. STEWART, *Secretary*.

FERGUSLIE THREAD WORKS,
    PAISLEY, *30th October, 1906*.

J. & P. COATS,

Dr.   **Balance Sheet at**

To Share Capital Authorised and Subscribed—
    250,000 6 per cent. Preference Shares of £10 each, fully paid,... £2,500,000 0 0
    £3,000,000 Preferred Ordinary Stock, fully paid, ... 3,000,000 0 0
    4,500,000 Ordinary Shares of £1 each, fully paid, ... 4,500,000 0 0
                                                                                   £10,000,000 0 0
,, Debenture Stock, at 3¾ per cent., ... 917,420 0 0

,, Interest on Debenture Stock, half-year to date, payable 1st July, ... £10,917,420 0 0
,, Dividend and Interest Warrants outstanding, ... 17,257 11 1
,, Sundry Trade Accounts, ... 378,855 17 8
,, Marine and Fire Underwriting Account,... ... ... 266,523 0 10
,, Reserve Fund, ... 350,471 15 3
,, Dividend Reserve Fund, ... 3,500,000 0 0
,, Pension Fund for Employees, ... £250,000 0 0   450,000 0 0
,, ,, ,, transferred to Central Agency, Ltd., 20,100 19 9
                                                                                        229,899 0 3
,, Suspense Account—Provision against depreciation of Investments, ... 185,096 0 6
,, Profit and Loss Account—
    Balance at Credit, as below, ... £2,974,088 9 4
    Balance from 30th June, 1905,... ... ... 479,908 8 8
                                                            £3,453,996 18 0
    Deduct—
Interest on Debenture Stock for the year,   £36,462 8 0
Dividend of 6 per cent. on Preference
  Shares, 3 per cent. paid 31st December;
  3 per cent., 30th June, ...   150,000 0 0
Quarterly Dividends on Preferred Ordinary
  Stock, 5 per cent. paid 31st December;
  5 per cent., 31st March; 5 per cent.,
  30th June, ...   450,000 0 0
Quarterly Dividends on Ordinary Shares,
  5 per cent. paid 31st December; 5 per
  cent., 31st March; 5 per cent., 30th June,   675,000 0 0
Income Tax paid, less retained, ...   92,204 9 10
Debenture Premium paid in excess of
  amount provided, ...   5,617 14 11
                                                     1,409,284 12 9
                                                                        2,044,712 5 3
                                                                      £18,340,235 10 10

Dr.   **Profit and Loss Account for**

To General Charges for Management Salaries, Legal Expenses, Fees of Directors,
  Auditors' Fees, etc., ... £46,970 8 6
,, Balance carried to Balance Sheet, ... 2,974,088 9 4

                                                                             £3,021,058 17 10

ARCHD. COATS, *Chairman.*   In accordance with the provisions of the Companies' Act, 1900,
W. P. STEWART, *Secretary.*   Shareholders that we have examined and compared this
                                      Balance Sheets and Returns received from The Central
                                      a true and correct view of the state of the Company's
                              PAISLEY, *30th October, 1906.*

LIMITED.

30th June, 1906. Cr.

By Capital Expenditure, including Goodwill and Property comprised in the original purchase in 1890; the Expenditure in carrying out the arrangements with other Companies, including Goodwill and Shares acquired therein and permanent Loans to those Companies; also Investments in Shares of other Subsidiary Companies—as per Balance Sheet of 30th June, 1905,	£9,741,761	12	2		
„ Additional Shares in Subsidiary Companies and other Capital Expenditure for year ending 30th June, 1906, ...	71,038	8	8		
	£9,812,800	0	10		
Less Depreciation on Ferguslie Thread Works for year to 30th June, 1906, ...£41,797 11 9					
Deduct Renewals and Transfers of Amounts previously reserved against Machinery at Ferguslie, now superseded, ... 6,366 4 5					
	35,431	7	4		
				£9,777,368	13 6
„ Book Debts, Agents' Balances, etc., after deducting estimated Discount and providing for Bad and Doubtful Debts, ...				1,229,239	9 8
„ Stock of Goods and Stores, ...				1,478,061	9 8
„ Cash at Bankers and in hand, ...				1,721,534	9 0
„ Bills Receivable, ...				646,943	10 2
„ Investments, Loans, and Advances against Mortgages, ...				2,569,785	6 3
„ Advances to Subsidiary Companies for Stock and Working Expenses, and Dividends declared but not received by this Company at the date of this Balance Sheet, ...				917,302	12 7
				£18,340,235	10 10

Year ended 30th June, 1906. Cr.

By Profit and Dividends for the year, including Dividends and Interest from Subsidiary Companies, and after making provision for Depreciation and Bad and Doubtful Debts,	£2,908,333	12 8
„ Rents, ...	6,630	11 5
„ Transfer Fees, ...	821	13 0
„ Interest, ...	105,273	0 9
	£3,021,058	17 10

we hereby certify that all our requirements as Auditors have been complied with, and we report to the Balance Sheet and the Profit and Loss Account with the Books and Vouchers at Paisley, as well as with the Agency, Limited, Branches, and Subsidiary Companies, and we are of opinion that the Balance Sheet exhibits affairs as shown by the Books.

TURQUAND, YOUNGS & CO., } Auditors.
DAVID W. KIDSTON,

REPORT AND ACCOUNTS

For the Year ended 30th June,
1906.

NOTICE IS HEREBY GIVEN that the SIXTEENTH ANNUAL ORDINARY GENERAL MEETING of J. & P. COATS, Limited, will be held in the MERCHANTS' HALL, 1 West George Street, Glasgow, *on Thursday, 29th November, 1906*, at Twelve o'Clock Noon, for the following purposes:—

1st.—To receive and consider the Profit and Loss Account and Balance Sheet to the 30th June, 1906, and the Report of the Directors and Auditors, and for other business of the Ordinary General Meeting.

2nd.—To elect Directors.

3rd.—To elect Auditors, and to fix their remuneration.

By Order of the Board,

W. P. STEWART,
Secretary.

FERGUSLIE THREAD WORKS,

The Reserve Fund could of itself pay the Preference fixed dividends, and a good commercial dividend on the Preferred and Ordinary Shares for many years, even if no profit whatever were being made during that time.

The dividend on the Ordinary Shares has been as follows:—

1897,	20 per cent.		
1898,	30 ,,		on £3,000,000.
1899,	30 ,,	and bonus of 10 %	
1900,	30 ,,	,, ,, 20 %	
1901,	20 ,,		Capital increased in 1901.
190?,	20 ,,		
1903,	20 ,,		£1 Shares—£4,500,000.
1904,	20 ,,		
1905,	20 ,,		
1906,	20 ,,	and bonus of 5 %	

Such results are unusual in industrial concerns, and have had some remarkable consequences. They produced quite a "boom" in industrial "combines." Investors lost their heads altogether, and promoters were not slow to gratify their demands. Combines of all sorts of impecunious firms were placed upon the market, and for a time almost anything could be floated. Ventures of the most dubious character were applied for, far in excess of the amounts required. But time brought about a startling revulsion. Not one of all these combines had the staying power of Coats. They quickly got into difficulties, and most of them had a long and weary road to travel on the good old lines of care and economy before they got out of the mess. It is not an unfair inference to draw, that the investing public dropped, at least for a time, as much in these ventures as had been gained by the remark-

COATS' MILLS AT FERGUSLIE.

able and legitimate success of the innocent cause of all this speculative mania.

The mills of the Coats Combination in Paisley cover a hundred acres of ground. They possess an aggregate engine force of thirty thousand horse power—requiring a daily consumpt of four hundred tons of coal—to drive half a million of spindles; and they give employment directly to over ten thousand persons, while thirty thousand may be taken as the total number of the employees of the Combination in all

CLARKS' MILLS AT SEEDHILLS.

countries. Of these, the majority are girls and women, ranging from fourteen years of age to fifty and more. The bobbin turning and dyeing departments are staffed exclusively by males.

The rate of pay is liberal. A girl who has just left school, at the age of fourteen, usually starts with a wage of about

6s. 6d. per week, advancing according to merit till 15s. per week is attained. 15s. may be taken as a fair average wage among the women; though, on the other hand, it has to be borne in mind there are others who receive as much as 36s. and 38s. per fortnight.

EAGLEY MILLS, BOLTON.

The male operatives begin work at fourteen years of age, start with 7s. per week, and gradually rise till their wages equal those of good tradesmen.

Work starts at 6 A.M. Breakfast from 9 to 10, dinner from 2 to 3, the labour of the day terminating at 6 P.M. The total working hours per week are fifty-five and a half.

The consumption of bobbin wood is enormous, and threatened at one time the practical deforestation of Scotland. Pirnmill, in Arran, marks the site of a saw mill which denuded the west coast of Arran of its fairy garniture of scrubby ashs and birks, and there were many such small mills scattered over the West Highlands. Scotland still contributes its share, but

Archibald Coats, Esq.,
Chairman of Messrs. J. & P. Coats, Limited.

the bulk of the wood now used in Paisley for the thread trade is imported from the North of Europe and from North America, and annually averages fifteen thousand tons, producing about two hundred and fifty millions of spools—a remarkable change from the time when James Clark ordered the spools by half a gross at a time, and carried them home in his coat pocket.

The present Directors of Messrs. J. & P. Coats, Limited, number nineteen. We reproduce the portrait of the Chairman, Archibald Coats, Esq., of Woodside.

To determine the degrees of merit justly due respectively to each of these gentlemen for the great results obtained, would be an impossible task, and invidious if it were possible. Among them were those who, by patient labour and business ability, created the conditions of success. There also was the genius capable of grasping the vast possibilities thus created, and the consummate skill required to carry out the great enterprise. Nothing succeeds like success, and large as was the price which they asked for the business, subsequent events have shown that the vendors might, like Lord Clive, be "astonished at their own moderation." The public were not long in putting a much higher value upon their purchase.

CHAPTER VIII

MANAGEMENT

THE arrangement of the mills is kept in touch with the latest advances. Changes and improvements are continually going on, the tendency being always towards diminished space and more rapid production. Thirty years ago the spindles ran about three thousand revolutions per minute; now they run from eight to ten thousand, and the space occupied is less. In the construction, and frequent reconstruction of parts of the mills, every attention is paid to the health and comfort of the workers, combined with efficiency and speed. Excellent ventilation, sanitation, and cleanliness characterize every part of the works. The newest inventions in machinery are considered, and, if found good, are readily adopted, no matter at what cost. All obsolete machinery has a short shrift. Electric lighting and driving are gradually superseding the older methods.

The serious risk of fire absorbs attention. Sprinklers, portable fire extinguishers, and buckets filled with water are installed all over the place, while an up-to-date fire engine—manned by the employees and under a professional fire-master—ensures prompt measures in case of emergency. Watchmen patrol the buildings all night, and their visits are automatically registered by a clock, so that no shirking of this essential inspection can take place without being discovered.

Accidents, especially to the fingers, are not uncommon, and in every room there is a Red Cross box, containing the necessary requisites for first aid. Attendance at ambulance classes is, in a manner, compulsory on the male workers.

HALF-TIMERS' SCHOOL, FERGUSLIE.

A large sum is set aside each year for the Pension Fund, which now amounts to over £200,000. From this fund all old and deserving workers are liberally provided for.

The two firms continue to take that lively interest in the welfare and education of the work-people, which was always practised by the worthy men who founded the industry. Evening classes are provided for the younger men, the attendance at which is in some degree compulsory, although the whole expense is paid by the firm. Lads of ability are transferred from these schools to the Technical College, where their progress is noted, and those who show aptitude are marked for promotion in the mills.

The education of the younger girls is provided for in the elegant Half-Timers' School, of which we give an illustration.

CRICKET FIELD, FERGUSLIE.

No expense has been spared in fitting up this commodious building, and although, owing to an alteration in the Education Act, it is not now absolutely necessary, it is maintained in the interest of the young people.

In a convenient meadow near to the Ferguslie works, ample accommodation is provided for tennis, cricket, and football games, where hundreds of the workers may be seen enjoying themselves in the summer evenings. Beautiful bowling greens, with suitable offices, have been formed convenient to both the Anchor and Ferguslie Mills, where the interest is maintained by much friendly rivalry.

Near to this field a number of model cottages in the English self-contained fashion have been built by the firm—

GIRLS' HOME, FERGUSLIE.

a style of dwelling which might with advantage be multiplied in Paisley.

For young girl workers who may reside at too great a distance, or who may not have the benefit of a home, a residence, under an experienced matron, has been built, where, for a limited payment, these young people can enjoy much home comfort.

Country and seaside excursions are also admirably organized. On the summer holiday—the "Sma' Shot Saturday" of the old weavers—the first Saturday of July, the thread workers have a trip, which they manage with wonderful ability and forethought. They generally arrange for six or seven different excursions, which frequently require two or three trains to each place. The younger girls are grouped together, sometimes numbering fifteen hundred, and on arrival at their destination they find everything arranged by some of the older hands. Ample refreshments are provided, and distributed in a well-ordered manner, according to the departments to which the workers belong. Tents are provided on the chance of bad weather. Music is abundant, and dancing and sports are carried on, and prizes given—amounting on some occasions to £30. The charge to each of the younger girls is merely nominal. As many as ten thousand trippers connected with the thread trade will sometimes enjoy a holiday in this manner. The workers make all the arrangements themselves, and long experience has qualified them well for this duty. A charge is made in every case, but the firm makes up any deficit.

Each of the flats has what is known as a "Holiday Bank." Weekly contributions are made to it by the thrifty girls, and one of their number is appointed banker. When the summer holiday season comes round, some of the girls will receive as much as £10 each. It is stated that sometimes £12,000 has been gathered in during the year — a remarkable illustration alike of good wages and of prudent economy.

The fair, and even generous, manner in which the thread firms have dealt with their workers, has had the usual excellent results. Good sense and friendly feeling have overcome with ease such difficulties as have arisen, and there never have been any protracted labour disputes. In a recent instance, a difference arose which required some time to adjust. The delay was not occasioned by any unwillingness to investigate and remedy any alleged grievance, but because of the possible far-reaching consequences of an unwise or hasty decision. The workers waited with becoming patience, and the revised rates, when decided, were made retrospective, so that some of the girls had as much as £15 to receive at the adjustment. This, no doubt, showed that the complaint was well founded, but it also showed the readiness of the firm to do perfect justice to their employees.

CHAPTER IX

BENEFACTIONS

THE leading men in the thread trade have at all times taken a lively interest in the welfare of the town. We frequently find them as members of the Town Council and Magistrates of the Burgh, and in several instances they have filled the office of Provost, and always with acceptance. But more particularly they have taken a special interest in, and freely given their personal services to, all projects for improving the condition of the people. Their names are to be found on the governing boards of every institution and society, educational, philanthropic and religious, in the town. During the dark days consequent upon the decay of the shawl trade, they did much to tide over the period of suffering through which the town passed, on its way to the present improved economic position. When success flowed in upon them, they dispensed their wealth with a liberal hand, and the town is enriched and adorned by many substantial evidences of their benefactions.

In the prosperous times of the weaving trade in Paisley, there was no pressing necessity for a Public Park. The town was not large, and the immediate neighbourhood abounded in delightful walks and charming country scenery. But as the town increased, and factories multiplied, the want of a park began to be much felt.

John Love (1747-1828), at one time a successful manufacturer, was an enthusiastic florist. He acquired about seven acres of land on the road to Inchinnan—the portion which is now called Love Street—and formed there the Hope Temple Gardens. Many valuable and interesting plants were collected, and the gardens were well stocked, and became a place of public resort.

Entrance to Hope Temple Gardens, 1866.

There was also included a Museum of geological and botanical specimens, which, in 1837, was under the care of Mr. William Small. But misfortune overtook the owner, and the estate went into the hands of trustees. The glory had departed; and, becoming known as Love's Folly, it was transformed into a market garden, where the children were accustomed to go for entertainment when the strawberries and gooseberries were ripe.

Offered for sale in 1866, it was bought privately by Mr. Thomas Coats of Ferguslie. He enclosed and re-arranged the whole place, built convenient waiting-rooms and a lodge, and erected a splendid fountain in the centre. The place was then named

The Fountain Gardens.

Fountain Gardens.

It was presented to the town by Mr. Coats, on 26th May, 1868, together with an endowment of £5,000, in order that it might be maintained for the good of the community, free of charge. This endowment was further augmented by his eldest son, Mr. James Coats, Junr., of Ferguslie, in 1892, by £3,000, and again, in 1901, by £2,000, so that the total endowment now amounts to £10,000.

This magnificent gift was only the forerunner of many more which the thread manufacturers have given to the town.

At the meetings of the Philosophical Institution, the desirableness of a town Museum was frequently expressed, but lack of

FREE PUBLIC LIBRARY AND MUSEUM.

funds prevented any action, till the problem was solved in an unexpected way. On 22nd January, 1867, it was announced that Mr. Peter Coats intended to build and present to the town a

Museum and Library.

The Libraries Act was adopted by the community on 28th March. 1867, and the building commenced in High Street, at an estimated cost of £15,000; but, as everything was done in the most substantial and complete manner, the ultimate cost must have been far beyond this limit.

The honour of knighthood was conferred upon Mr. Peter Coats on 2nd July, 1869. The building was transferred to the Town Council on 23rd September, 1870, on which occasion Sir Peter made a speech which breathes such a noble spirit that we subjoin a few passages. He said :—

"The Museum and Library I have conjoined, because I regard them as appropriately related to one another. The Museum is in many respects the complement of the Library—they are intended to be mutually helpful. For example, the standard works in the Reference Library, say in Botany, Geology, or other branches of Natural History, will be all the more practically valuable when there are specimens and exactly systematized collections in the Museum to illustrate what has been published ; and, conversely, the specimens and collections will be more useful when the best writers in accessible works explain their history, their qualities, and the relations by which they are generalized. (Applause.) Of course, Natural History is too wide a field for anything like exhaustive illustration by a provincial Museum such as ours; but the study of each branch can be best prosecuted, in the first instance, through what is local, or nearest at hand, and, therefore, it is that I expect a creditable representation of the chief features of the Natural History of Renfrewshire. (Applause.) The industrial products, manufactures, and antiquities, may also be adequately represented; and I think it is of importance, now that the Science and Art Department is extending its examinations over Britain, that diagrams, as well as chemical and other apparatus, be at hand in the Museum, that it may be a centre of beneficial influence, to be modified or extended according to circumstances. (Loud applause.) The Reference Library is closely connected with the Museum, and is separated from the General Library, that distraction may be avoided. My aim is that the poorest youth may have access to the best books in his effort at self-improvement—that the mechanic, the artist, the Sabbath-school teacher, the missionary, and the student in the University, may find in it assistance. (Applause.) The General Library, which will supply books for family reading, has been suitably furnished by me, with a view to young men, and the aged and the infirm, spending in it unoccupied hours, and with a view also specially to its being a home for thoughtful men in those dull days when there is no employment, and the temptation often is strong to seek stimulants that only leave him sadder and poorer. (Applause.) I sincerely hope that, in this way, it may prove a blessing by promoting temperance, sobriety, and self-respect."

In 1882, Sir Peter Coats made extensive additions to the Free Library and Museum, adding a Picture Gallery, new Reference Library Room, and enlarged Museum space; and, in 1904, his eldest son, Mr. James Coats (now Sir James) of Auchendrane, still further extended it. This most recent addition enabled the Directors to provide space for a permanent display of the beautiful harness shawls, for which Paisley has earned a great reputation. A Loan Exhibition of these and similar fabrics was held in June, 1905, and attracted much attention. The success of that Exhibition, which led to the permanent collection, was largely due to the personal exertions and generosity of Mr. John Robertson and Mr. Robert Cochran, both of whom have a hereditary interest

SHAWL EXHIBITION.

in this now vanished industry. The present collection, which is unique of its kind, has been enriched by liberal donations of shawls and printed fabrics from a large number of ladies and gentlemen in the town.

The Free Library contains over 37,000 volumes, and the annual issues number about 80,000. It has been augmented by many costly gifts, among which may be mentioned the beautifully illuminated Ashburton MSS. of the fifteenth century, valued at

£1,200, presented by Mr. Archibald Coats of Woodside, a son of Sir Peter Coats.

Mr. Thomas Coats always took a special interest in scientific pursuits, and was a steady supporter of the Philosophical Institution. This Society, which was founded in 1808, had, like all such institutions, its periods of prosperity and of adversity. The late Rev. William Fraser, D.D., minister of the Free Middle Church, an earnest and accomplished student of science, did much to awaken interest in educational and scientific work, and the brothers Coats were early associated with these efforts. The want of instruments was felt to be a hindrance to study, and Mr. Thomas Coats, always liberal, presented a telescope to the Institution. This instrument was afterwards replaced by one of greater power, and, in the end, Mr. Coats crowned his gifts by the erection of

The Coats Observatory.

This building, after being splendidly equipped, was transferred, on 18th October, 1882, to the Philosophical Institution, together with an endowment of £2,000. Mr. Thomas Coats died on 15th October, 1883, but his family continued to take a warm interest in the Observatory, and his Trustees added £2,000 to the endowment on 14th March, 1884. In 1892, Mr. James Coats, Junr., of Ferguslie, further extended the buildings of the Observatory, adding many valuable instruments, and increasing the endowment by £2,000; and again in 1898 by a further sum of £4,000, so that the entire endowment now amounts to £10,000.

COATS OBSERVATORY.

The Philosophical Institution has continued to do good work, and among its best friends and most earnest workers was the late Rev. Andrew Henderson, LL.D., F.R.A.S., minister of Abbey Close United Presbyterian Church.

Mr. Thomas Coats, being an engineer, naturally interested himself, as we have said, in scientific and educational matters, and was a liberal supporter of all efforts in this direction. And here the writer of these pages may be forgiven for relating an incident—the only occasion on which he had any intercourse with a member of the Coats family.

In those early days, before the repeal of the taxes on knowledge, a newspaper cost fourpence halfpenny, and did not contain as much matter as those now sold for a halfpenny. The price was too high for working people, and reading rooms were established. One of these was the Artizans' Institution, which occupied part of a building which stood on the exact spot where now the statue of Thomas Coats is placed. This Institution, of which Mr. Coats was a warm friend, besides providing newspapers, established evening classes, and held examinations in connection with the Society of Arts, so paving the way for the advent of that technical education now considered so essential. Mr. Thomas Coats was chairman of the local committee charged with the examinations. Dr. W. B. M'Kinlay, a well-known medical practitioner of that time, offered a prize of a Society of Arts microscope to the young members of the Artizans' Institution for the best essay "On the benefits of scientific education to the artizan." The present writer, then a young lad, was the winner of this prize. It was presented by Mr. Coats at a public meeting on 16th September, 1861, Dr. M'Kinlay remarking that he had read the essay with interest, and commended it to the notice of the young men. The attention thus early drawn to the subject of technical education was not without results. The writer, in after years, was one of the founders—and for some time Chairman—of

ARTIZANS' INSTITUTION.

The Incorporated Weaving, Dyeing, and Printing College of Glasgow, the leading technical institution in Scotland in connection with the textile industry.

On the passing of the Scotch Education Act, the interest which Mr. Thomas Coats had always taken in educational matters was acknowledged by his townsmen in electing him the first Chairman of the School Board, an office which he held till his lamented death in 1883.

Mr. Coats was unceasing not only in his labours but in his generosity. He gave a donation of £4,000 in order that the first four new schools, then being built, should have twelve feet of air space per pupil in place of eight feet. In the Report for 1877, it is stated that, in consequence of this gift, "The sanitary results have already proved gratifying. By the wise restriction which the benevolence of Mr. Coats has imposed as a condition of his grant of £4,000, the teachers and the children not only enjoy more space for work, but breathe purer air. . . . The principal teachers of the new schools bear unqualified testimony to the greater healthfulness of the pupil teachers and the scholars, as resulting from the special arrangement giving more air space."

In 1876, he also presented increased playground accommodation for the George Street (or West) School, at considerable cost. By his tact and business ability, no less than by the conspicuous sincerity of purpose, he greatly facilitated the work of the School Board.

The Technical College and School of Art received from Messrs. J. & P. Coats a free site, of great value, in George Street, and a donation of £3,000; to which Mr. James Coats, Junr., of Ferguslie, added £500, and other members of the family also gave considerable sums.

Clark Town Hall.

The want of a Public Hall had long been felt in Paisley, and several unsuccessful attempts had been made to erect such a building. During 1872, largely by the exertions of Mr. James

GEORGE A. CLARK TOWN HALL.

Clark of Chapel House, subscriptions were obtained which, on 8th February, 1873, amounted to £13,870 10s. 6d. On 10th March, 1873, it was announced that Mr. George A. Clark, of Newark, New Jersey, had left a legacy of £20,000 to build a Town Hall for his native town.

The human interest and sympathy with the work people which have always marked the thread manufacturers is nowhere better illustrated than by a condition attached to this gift. That was the stipulation that there must be a large reading room for working men, where they could sit in comfort and enjoy a smoke, and that the room should be open from five o'clock in the morning until twelve o'clock at night. Mr. Clark had a warm heart to the working man.

On 8th June, the members of the Clark family intimated that they would prefer to undertake the whole expense of erecting the hall to the memory of their deceased relative; a promise which they fulfilled in a princely manner. The subscription list was then closed, and the money returned. A prominent site in the New Town, at the corner of the Old or St. James' Bridge, was acquired for £9,000, and the erection commenced of the palatial buildings which now adorn this part of the town. The cost of this superb structure has been estimated at not less than £110,000.

What with the preliminary arrangements and other unforeseen delays, it took nearly ten years to complete the work. The foundations alone, being so near the river bank, must have absorbed a vast sum. The building was handed over to the Corporation on 30th January, 1882. The large hall rivals in beauty and convenience any similar structure in the West of Scotland, and the various smaller halls are in keeping with it.

Connected with these gifts to the town by the thread manufacturers, may be mentioned

The Coats Memorial Church.

COATS MEMORIAL CHURCH.

Although not a gift to the community, it is a great ornament to the town. It is attached to the Baptist denomination, and was erected to the memory of Mr. Thomas Coats by his family.

It is an exquisite structure of geometrical Gothic architecture, with a central tower which corresponds well with its monumental character. The interior is rich in carvings. The alabaster pulpit, the marble baptistry, the carved oak stalls, and the great organ together make this one of the most beautiful ecclesiastical

PULPIT OF COATS MEMORIAL CHURCH.

edifices in the country. The cost is understood to have been between £100,000 and £150,000.

The style of building, with its high arched roof, is favourable to musical effects, and in accordance with its resemblance to an English Cathedral, the service has been made slightly more ornate than is usual in Scotland, while the quality of the pulpit utterances has been maintained at a high intellectual level.

The Royal Alexandra Infirmary.

This institution has always received the hearty support of the whole community. The employers give large annual subscriptions for maintenance, the workmen of many firms in the town send annual contributions, and a substantial sum is raised annually by the proceeds of a concert held at "The

ROYAL ALEXANDRA INFIRMARY.

Glen," which happily commemorates Paisley's much loved poet, Robert Tannahill.

When it was found necessary to remove from the site in Bridge Street, which it had long occupied, to a more open space in what is now called the Barbour Park, a large Building Fund was required. While keen interest was evinced by the whole town in this good work, the thread manufacturers were conspicuous for their munificence, and this in addition to the large sums which they annually subscribed for maintenance.

The firm of J. & P. Coats, Limited, contributed to the Building Fund in 1903 a special donation of £3,000, on conditions, which were complied with, and which resulted in an additional sum of £3,750 being obtained from other subscribers.

A Bazaar to liquidate the debt on the buildings and for other purposes was held, and participated in by all classes of the people. The young men got up private theatrical entertainments, and the thread mill girls did work for the Bazaar in many ways, including the making of toffee, which they sold for the benefit of the institution.

In addition to this, the thread manufacturers were conspicuous for the special gifts which they bestowed upon the Infirmary. Among these, Mr. Peter Coats of Garthland Place, a son of Sir Peter Coats, takes a high place. Mr. Coats, as a Director, had long taken an active part in the management, and by his generosity had assisted the Directors over many a difficulty, and enabled them to make the Infirmary one of the most complete in the country.

He undertook responsibility for the cost of the West Pavilion and Chapel, and built a block which is set apart for infectious diseases, thus greatly assisting the organization and working of the institution. He further erected the beautiful and complete Nurses' Home, which stands apart in the grounds of the Infirmary. It contains accommodation for all the nurses, and is fitted up with an elegance and refinement such as Mr. Coats considered was appropriate to the devoted ladies who form the nursing staff. He also cleared away much old property which overlooked the Infirmary on the south-east side, thereby adding to the amenity and openness of the situation.

Even these gifts did not exhaust his generosity to this deserving institution. He was the means, by a donation of £3,000, of founding "The Paisley Sick Relief Fund," which is

Nurses' Home.

administered by the Directors, and has been of much benefit to many unfortunate sufferers.

At a meeting of the subscribers and others interested in the Infirmary, held on 9th March, 1900, Mr. Peter Coats was appointed Honorary Life President, in recognition of what he had done for the institution.

Mr. James Coats, Junr., of Ferguslie House, in addition to his many gifts for other objects in the town, has shown great liberality to the Infirmary. His contributions to the Building

Fund amounted to many thousand pounds, and he presented a complete electric installation, besides furnishings and fittings for almost every department of the building. Other members of the Coats' family also contributed most generously to the institution.

Mr. John Clark of Gateside, 1827-1894.

The Clark family have been equally active in such good deeds, and have made many munificent gifts to the Infirmary. The late Mr. John Clark of Gateside left a legacy of £10,000 to the Endowment Fund of this institution. The James Clark Bequest Fund for Consumptive Patients, administered by the Directors, has benefitted to the extent of £10,000 in gifts from the late Mr. James Clark of Ralston, and the late Mr. John Clark of Gateside.

The Annie Clark Fund for Incurables, also managed by the Directors, was founded by Mrs. Stewart Clark of Kilnside, now of Dundas Castle, Linlithgowshire, and amounts to £12,000, contributed by herself and her husband. Mr. Stewart Clark endowed two beds at a cost of £2,500, and Mrs. Kerr of Gallowhill, a sister of Mr. Clark, endowed a bed at a cost of £1,250.

Mr. James Clark of Ralston, 1821-1881.

Mr. Kenneth M. Clark furnished the Operating Theatre, which probably involved an outlay of £500 to £1,000. In the history of the institution there have been frequent occasions when, from unforeseen causes, the expenditure has been unusually large. On one such occasion Mr. Kenneth M. Clark donated £1,000, and on another Mr. James Coats, Junr., gave a sum sufficient to wipe out the deficit.

The ladies of the thread connection have been liberal in donations of musical instruments of various sorts, and there have been minor gifts, which it is unnecessary to detail.

The present much respected Chairman of the Board of Directors of the Infirmary is Mr. Robert Balderston of Ardgowan, who has had a lifelong connection with the thread trade.

MR. ROBERT BALDERSTON, CHAIRMAN OF INFIRMARY.

Other institutions in the town, while not specially built by the thread manufacturers, have been largely supported by them.

The Paisley Industrial School has received many gifts from the thread manufacturers, notably by a legacy of £5,000 left by the late Mr. John Clark of Gateside, and £1,000 given by Mr. Stewart Clark, who had long taken an active interest in this institution, as well as in the Infirmary.

The Gleniffer Home for Incurables, Meikleriggs.

This building owes its existence mainly to the anxious care of Mrs. Archibald Coats of Woodside, a benevolent lady who has left a fragrant memory. The same estimable lady took an active interest in the Paisley Branch of the Scotch Girls' Society.

GLENIFFER HOME FOR INCURABLES.

After her lamented decease, a number of her friends in commemoration of her labours built

The Mrs. Archibald Coats Memorial Home,

in New Street, and connected it with the Scotch Girls' Friendly Society. This structure must have cost about £5,000.

In the same way many other benevolent institutions and churches in town have been liberally supported by the thread manufacturers, and, indeed, it may be said they have assisted almost every project for the public good in Paisley and the West of Scotland which has been proposed for the last two generations.

As to the private benevolences, of which no estimate can ever be made, it is sufficient to say that they have been on a royal scale. The poor, the feeble, the unfortunate, the widow and the orphan, have ever received a helpful hand; and, as these gifts have been continuous over the lifetime of several generations, and by a great number of generous men and women, it may be possible that the unseen and unrecorded liberality of the thread manufacturers has been greater even than that shown in so many permanent memorials of enduring stone which they have erected in the town.

The difficult problem of how to assist the needy without demoralizing them, has had to be faced, and although, no doubt, results have not in every case been what was desired, it may safely be said that an admirable discretion has presided over the distribution of this well-earned wealth. It has ever been employed to knit together, in the bonds of mutual sympathy and help, the various classes of the people; and the duties, as well as the rights of wealth, have been well understood and recognized.

CHAPTER X

OLD PAISLEY

TO one whose lot it has been to live during part of the two periods in the history of Paisley—so remarkable and so contrasted as those of the shawl trade and the thread trade—many interesting, and even pathetic, memories are awakened.

Writers who describe Paisley in the prosperous days of the shawl trade, make mention of the crowds of girls who issued at meal times from the warehouses. They were all clad in grey duffel cloaks with hoods which obscured their faces, and excited the curiosity of the amorous youths of the town. A local bard of the time sang of them—

> "My mither says, 'My son,
> Ye are lucky soon begun
> With the lassies for to run,
> With their grey cloaks on.'"

Duffel was a soft woollen cloth of the texture of flannel. The name is Dutch, and doubtless the fabric came originally from the Low Countries, as did the linen thread which preceded that of Bargarran.

By the time of which we are now treating (1840-1850), the duffel cloaks had passed away, and with them the stately old gentlemen who then occupied the Causeyside. There still, however, remained some relics of these old times, and the portrait of Alexander Carlile (p. 58) gives a fair idea of the costume of the period. The knee breeches had gone, but the chimney-pot hat of large dimensions, the clean-shaven face, the tail coat—now only used by waiters and for evening dress—and the ruffled shirt front still lingered; and the silver snuff box was always the first thing brought out on meeting a friend. It was usual to see, dangling under the vest, a bunch of seals attached to a massive gold chain. If one asked the time of day, the chain drew up from the subterranean depths of a fob pocket, as from a well, a watch approaching the size of a small turnip—popularly known to the boys as a "ticker," because the sound thereof might almost be heard on the other side of the street. These seals, glittering with cairngorms, were not altogether without use. Gummed envelopes and note paper had not yet come in. Letters were written on a double sheet of large paper, and folded, wafered, and sealed. The scratching of quills made an irritating sound in the counting houses, till Joseph Gillott, with his steel pens, drove them out. The quill pen, the wafer, and the sealing wax went out together, and carried the seals with them.

The shawl trade centred in the little stretch of Causeyside from the foot of St. Mirren Street to Forbes Street, and along that street to the River Cart. St. Mirren Street was then a steep and narrow lane, called the Water Wynd, and

Gilmour Street was blocked at the Cross by a building, alongside of which was a passage named the "Hole in the Wa'."

St. Mirren Street, 1865.

In Causeyside, in those days, might be seen old Robert Kerr—with his gold spectacles, cheery face, and active step—come over from Thread Street to buy some Thibet yarn or spun silk, with the various quantities written on scraps of paper at the bottom of his capacious hat, held in place by the inevitable bandanna handkerchief, so indispensable to all snuffers.

John Morgan, dapper little gentleman, might be standing on his door-step, looking down the street, if peradventure a buyer should turn the corner of the Bank of Scotland at the foot of the Water Wynd, and wondering if the visitor would be waylaid by Whitehill or Walker, or, if he should escape so great a danger, would he get past Cumberland Court, with Charles Burgess standing at the close-mouth ; for Morgan's warehouse was well up the street?

There, too, were the brothers James and John Robertson, with their genial smile and pleasant words of greeting to everyone ; and old Thomas Risk of the Western Bank—the offices of which were at the corner of Forbes Street—little dreaming of the great disaster that was to overtake this important institution. There also might be James Forbes, of Forbes & Hutchison, a stately, reserved, and handsome man ; and Archibald Hutchison, his partner, alert and bustling; or Archie Harper, with his leonine locks and merry glance, than whom, none knew better how to manage those buyers who liked to complete a bargain by an adjournment up to "Peter's." William Abercrombie, a handsome blue-eyed Saxon, and his partner, John Yuill, a dark-eyed Celt. Robert F. Dalziel and Alexander Begg, who united artistic taste with good manufacturing ; and Matthew Scott, on his way to a meeting at the Infirmary or the Ragged School. Then gentle David Speirs, with head inclined, moving quietly along, dreaming of those exquisite designs in shawls, for which his firm was famous; and burly Robert Rowat, stumping down the street, taking up the whole breadth of the pavement, to the terror of all small boys, and the amusement of those half-witted loafers, who relieved the tedium of the Causeyside.

St. Mirren Street, 1906.

There among the yarn and cloth merchants would be Provost Philips, refined, courteous and cultured; and Provost Pollock, a useful man in his day, and a choice *raconteur*; and John M. Symington, deep in all religious and educational movements; and Hugh Brown, with his anxious enquiring face, limping along. Then John Greenlees, turning upon you alternately his blue eye and his brown one, a representative of a family connected for several generations with the textile trade of the town.

The genial Laird of Glenfield also (the last to sport the ruffled shirt front) would be there, looking after the finishing, so that the orders might not all go to Aikman. One remembers with pleasure his clear-cut face and fund of pawky humour; and also the Irish car, drawn by his piebald pony "Batty," on which the "kind auld laird" was ever ready to give a "lift" to a weary wayfarer. Among dyers, there would be Howard Lang, sonsie William Craw, and P. C. Macgregor, a man of marked personality, and many others who might be named.

There, too, later on, was David Gilmour, the best narrator of weaver stories that Paisley has produced. It was easy to see from the merry twinkle in his eye, and from his quaint conversation, how much he appreciated and was quietly studying the interesting characters of those days. There, also, snuff-box in hand, might have been seen William M'Intyre of Colinslee Print Works, talking with Robert Guthrie, James M'Murchy or James Millar of Whitehill's. Some of the printed shawls were very popular, rivalling in beauty the harness work, and at one time there were at least ten printworks in the vicinity. Colinslee alone employed over a thousand workers, and on the other side of the town, Messrs. Walker, Drybrough & Co., at Arkleston, did then and do still maintain, the reputation of the district for this class of work.

Perhaps there would be a noise, and looking around, there

was the "Charleston Drum" (fortunately still preserved), coming down the street accompanied by a group of weavers, led by that enthusiastic Radical, Colin Black, and followed by all the ragged weans of the neighbourhood, hurrahing with great glee at the demonstration to be made, and effigy to be burned, before the warehouse of some "wee cork," who had presumed to break the table of prices. And there, too, would be Richard Watson

BANK OF SCOTLAND, OLD CAUSEYSIDE, 1865.

to put it all in the *Paisley Herald* next Saturday; and our "ever green and perpetual" Provost Murray, well named the "Provost of Scotland," not disliking a little fun, but anxious that there should be no breach of the peace. Now they are gone, all gone "these old familiar faces," leaving behind them only a delightful memory.

Nothing could be done in Paisley in those days without poetry, or, at least, rhyme—more or less lame in the feet. One of the bards exclaims—

> "Hark, hark to the sound of the Charleston Drum!
> 'Tis the champions of liberty—onward they come;
> They're to meet in their strength down in the Old Low,
> And the'ill soon show the Provost the way for to go."

Another follows in the same strain—

> "If a Causeyside 'cork' tried the table tae smash,
> The Charleston weavers came down on him crash;
> They turned oot in hunners, determined tae win,
> And marched doon Causeyside wi' their Charleston Drum.

> "The 'cork' grew quite frichtit when he heard the big drum,
> An' saw the great crood, full o' mischief an' fun,
> So he promised, in future, to pay the full sum;
> Then they marched back in triumph wi' the Charleston Drum."

But life is not all "cakes and ale." There was another side to the picture. The shawl trade was subject to periods of great depression, and at times many decent families were brought nearly to starvation. Soup kitchens were required almost every winter, and bread riots were not uncommon. Privation brought disease. Smallpox and fever were constantly more or less present, while the dreaded cholera made occasional visits. There were no ambulance waggons then, but the trestle bed of the Infirmary, with the red and white striped curtains, borne by two men, scared the little children playing in the street, and made them cover their noses, notwithstanding the bits of camphor in a little bag, which every careful mother had hung round their necks.

Of this time of sorrow the writer had his share, for many of his people were operative weavers. As the distress deepened, households were broken up, playmates and school companions were forced to leave the town. Some went to the wilds of Canada, many to the California gold diggings, then just dis-

PAISLEY ABBEY FROM CAUSEYSIDE, 1830.
From a drawing by Mr. J. Cook, grandfather of Mr. William Cook, "Gazette" Office.

covered, and some to Australia and New Zealand. Others, and the writer among the number, went no further afield than to Glasgow. But even that seemed a foreign land to the Paisley man. It was never "home." The people were in many respects different, and much as experience has taught us to admire the splendid business qualities of the Glasgow people, they are not our "ain folk." Perhaps if they were not just so conspicuously able and successful, we would like them better.

Then, as the years rolled on, the writer came back in the hope of ending his days among the scenes of his youth. But it was like a rude awakening from a dream. No emigrant who had spent forty years in a foreign land and returned to the

East Side of Causeyside, 1892.

old home, could have been more astonished. Everything was changed. His school companions were nearly all gone. Some had moved west to elegant villas in the new suburb of Castlehead, but the greater number had found quiet resting-places in Woodside Cemetery. Instead of the old, dreamy town, everywhere now was bustle. A new heaven and a new earth, wherein all was business--business! Wide, and widening streets. The clang-clanging of tram-car bells resounded in the principal thoroughfares, and crowds of eager people pushed along the streets. Palatial public and private buildings appeared on every hand. In vain the wanderer listened for the click of the shuttle from one of those plain two-storied houses, with the "through-gawn" close, the outside stair, and the "yaird" behind, where the wearied workman could "rax" his limbs

THE "CHARLESTON DRUM."

amidst the scent of sweet briar and spearmint. It was easy to be neighbourly with two families on the stair-head and the mid-room perhaps tenanted by some gentle spinster, who wound pirns or fringed shawls, and marched off on Sundays—clad in a harness plaid, with her Bible wrapped in a napkin, and enclosing a sprig of "apple ringie" to mark the place—to some church, of which she was one of the "stoops."

Then the bleaching greens were gone; those delightful

scenes of feminine gossip over the hedge. No longer can we see the thrifty housewife gaily spreading out the fragrant linens to the sun, for now the smoke renders bleaching impossible, and everything has to be sent to the steam laundry.

Now everywhere there are four-storied lands, ashlar fronts, oriel windows, tiled passages, hot and cold water—no more

"Peter's," 1901.

stoups to carry from the well—and ten families on one common stair. "Neebours" there are none. The occupants are too many for companionship, and all are eager after their own business, and have no time for a stair-head crack or an exchange of friendship.

A generation of children has arisen who never knew the delight of hurrahing as a cart of coal was shot down at the close mouth. That grand event never occurs now, for coal houses no longer exist, and the weekly supply is carried up in bags.

Then the candy-man, with his barrow ornamented with whirling paper flags, now rarely delights the children. How can we ever forget the time when, in exchange for some "ravellins," old bones, or rags, he would give us a bit of his toothsome "blackman," gouged out with a rusty knife from a

"Peter's," 1906.

not too clean old tin tray? It was delicious. Not even " Teugh Geordie"—a noted confectioner of the Townhead— could make anything finer, and compared with this the modern toffee, wrapped up in tinsel paper to make it acceptable, is quite insipid. But now he and his retinue of rejoicing youngsters would be in imminent danger of their lives from some motor car fleeing along—vehicles, by the way, now largely made in the town. We had smells in Paisley in the old times, some of them pungent enough down Sneddon way, but the stench of the new motor car eclipses them all.

Then the pavements are now laid with concrete—no doubt a great improvement for the girls to play "pal-als," and fine for slides on frosty days—but the boys can no longer play at the "bools" as on earth pavements, where holes could be made, and where were those delightful uncertainties and hazards which would now train the eye for future feats in golf!

Where, also, is the "Jail Square," with its collection of dirty fish barrows and empty barrels, round the wooden booth of Willie Shaw? He of the "pluckie" face is gone, and with him his savoury "Bervies" and dried, strong-tasting "Speldrins," which went well with a bit of oat cake, and had the additional advantage—appreciated by the knowing ones—of concealing the smell of a dram. But why talk of drams? The "Change Houses" also are gone. We cannot now find those humble "howffs," where honest, if drouthy, cronies on raw days could step into a low-roofed room, with a cheerful fire, and feel the hospitable "crunching" of the feet on the sanded floor, and be served with "a wee gill of the best" by the buxom widow, with the drugget apron in front, and the tartan shawl crossed over her ample bosom and tied in a bunch behind. Here one could have a canny crack about what "new mischief thae blasted Tories in London were up to again."

Now all these are gone, and in their place at every corner are to be found flaring gin palaces, brilliant in plate glass, polished wood, and glittering brass—but no fireside, no pleasant welcome, and no quiet corner to sit down; in fact, generally no seats at all; only a high counter at which to stand and imbibe as fast as possible the vile stuff, and incontinently be turned out into the street.

Mr. James E. Christie, Artist.

Thus the old, dreamy Paisley, with its quaint ways, is slowly drifting away into a vague past, surrounded by those dim shadows which, obscuring the defects, leave behind only a radiance of pleasant recollections.

As illustrative of Old Paisley, we have the pleasure of reproducing the well-known portrait picture of the "Paisley Cross, 1868," painted by our distinguished artist and townsman, Mr. James E. Christie, and now, by the liberality of the late Sir Peter Coats, preserved in the Art Gallery of the Free Public Library and Museum.

PAISLEY CROSS, 1868, BY MR. JAMES E. CHRISTIE.

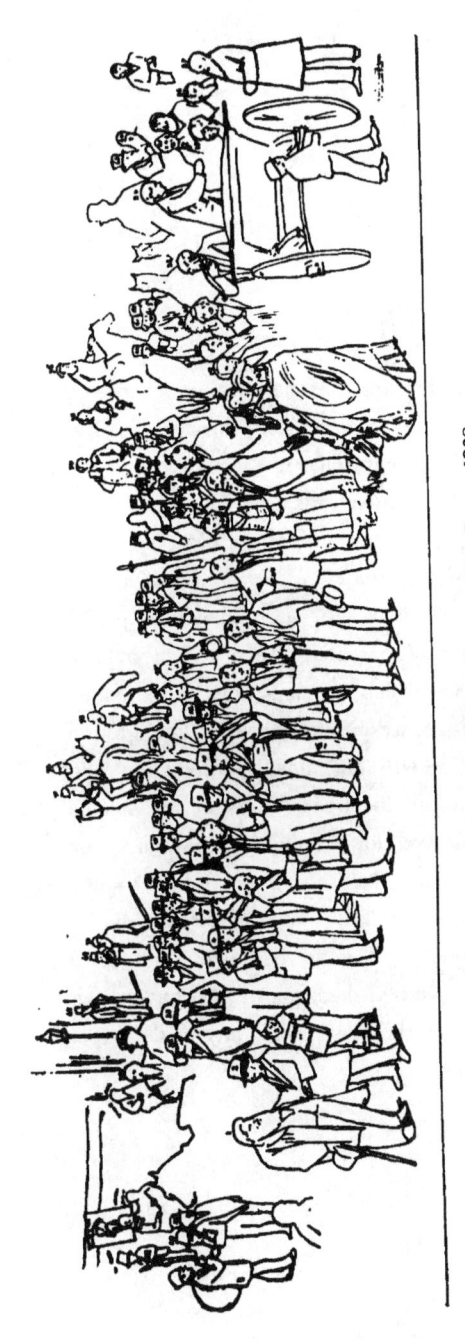

KEY TO PORTRAITS IN PAISLEY CROSS, 1868.

CHAPTER XI

TRANSITION

A RAMBLE round Paisley for the purpose of observing the changes which have taken place during the last fifty or more years, may begin naturally at the Cross, and the prominent feature here is, or rather was, the Steeple. This building was erected in 1757 on the site of an older structure which had shown signs of decay. To the north stood the tolbooth or jail, the front of which was adorned with a piazza supported by two square, rustic arched pillars. The outside stair led to a platform from which proclamations were made, and where prisoners were exposed in the stocks. The ground floor of the steeple was called "the howff," where ale and porter were sold. The rooms in the upper floors of the steeple and the tolbooth were reserved for criminals, and it may be noted that every prisoner incarcerated for a night had to pay the jailer a fee of fourpence, but if he were a burgess of the town he got off for twopence. It is to be hoped that Lord Brougham and the other distinguished men who have been presented with the freedom of the town were duly made aware of this important concession.

The lower floor of the tolbooth was occupied by the Council Chamber and other municipal offices; the floor above, reached by the outside stair, was the Sheriff Court House.

CROSS STEEPLE AND TOLLBOOTH, 1757.

On the removal of the Council business to the new County Buildings in County Square, the tolbooth was taken down in 1821, and replaced by an addition made to the Saracen's Head

Inn, which, under the name of the Town's House, had been built by the Town Council, in 1751, as a place of public entertainment. The Saracen's Head Inn had a large ball-room

CROSS STEEPLE AND SARACEN'S HEAD INN, 1868.

attached, and was for many years the principal hotel in the town. Being at the Cross, it was greatly frequented on market days, when it rang with the eloquence of bailies and councillors, besides buyers and sellers of all sorts, who in those days always made a market day a time of high festival. One of our many local rhymsters describes the scene as follows:—

Cross Steeple, 1870.

"When out and in the farmers drive,
And all is bustle and alive,
When waiters with a pinch contrive
   The guests to please,
In hundreds swarming, like a hive
   Of wasps or bees.

"Three farmers, tenants, all at will,
In hard-up circumstances still,
There sit, consulting, o'er a gill,
   What scheme or prank
Would get another new wind-bill
   Pass'd thro' the bank.

CROSS BEFORE DEMOLITIONS, 1906.

"A merchant jamb'd, sits farther ben,
'Tween Miller Muir and Baker Glen,
Upright, unquestionable men,
   A thousand ways,
But, boys who never sell their hen
   On rainy days."

The Paisley Burns Club, of which Tannahill was secretary, held its meetings here, and Professor John Wilson ("Christopher

North") and many other distinguished men have been present on memorable occasions at meetings in this renowned hostelry.

But what lingers most pleasantly in the memory is the Town's House stair. Well do we remember the steep double stair, with the polished mahogany hand-rails, which led up to

"Hole in the Wa'," 1836.

the public rooms on the upper floor. It was a ploy of the boys, whenever the waiter was out of sight, to sit astride on the double rail, and enjoy a glorious slide down to the bottom. This was one of the joys of Old Paisley which the new generation can never experience.

In 1868, a subsidence of the steeple, to the south, took place, in consequence of a sewer being formed a few feet from its foundation. The *Paisley Gazette* commemorated the event in the following lines :—

> "The town was filled with terror when we heard that, through an error
> In the giving of an order for the cutting of a sewer,
> And the mining and the sapping, and the pickaxing, and rapping
> By the workmen who were tapping a damp cellar or a store,
> To rid it of the water there—some two feet or more—
> Our old steeple might fall o'er, by this digging we deplore."

St. Mirren Street, 1906.

After it had stood for two years supported by wooden props (p. 129), the steeple was taken down, notwithstanding an unsuccessful attempt to interdict the work by Mr. John Crawford, writer—a well-known and somewhat original character of those days, and who is credited with the statement that "there is no philosophy without a 'dawnie.'" The bell of the steeple was cracked while being rung on the occasion of the

St. Mirren Street (Water Wynd), 1865.

marriage of the Prince of Wales—the present King Edward VII.—in 1863. After having served the town for two hundred and fifteen years, it was recast, and is still doing duty in the Lylesland United Free Church.

The block which formed the north side of the Cross (p. 130), and which has recently been removed—largely by the liberality of Mrs. John Polson of Westmount—so as to improve the square, has a historic interest for the older inhabitants. Here,

Diel's Elbow, 1865.

up an outside stair, was the Commercial Hotel, first Gibb's and afterwards Hinshelwood's, a rival to the Saracen's Head over the way, and also a great resort on market days. This hotel was greatly patronized on Sunday evenings by lads and lasses, after being at church and having had a walk. They wound up the night's enjoyment by an hour in the Commercial, where ale was the usual refreshment; tea being expensive in those days. Among all the changes that have taken place, nothing is more striking than that of the way in which such places as Gibb's flourished and did a roaring trade on Sunday nights, compared with the present quiet aspect of our public houses and hotels.

CORNER OF FORBES STREET, 1893.

Underneath the Commercial Hotel was Paton's drapery and hosiery shop, with the golden lamb over the door, admired by all Paisley boys; and next to it was the bookseller's shop and library of Motherwell, the brother of the poet. This range of buildings was continued eastwards to within a few feet of the Coffee Room (now the Savings Bank), and a narrow passage, called the "Hole in the Wa'," led through into Gilmour Street (p. 131). The obstructing block, with the crow-stepped gable, was removed about 1845, when Gilmour Street, which had been formed some time previously, was opened up from the Cross to the County Square. The corner of the "Hole in the Wa'" was the rendezvous of the recruiting sergeant, who, with his hat trimmed with streaming, gaudy ribbons, gave animation and

GORDON'S LOAN, 1901.

colour to the scene. The Coffee Room is a simple but elegant building of classic architecture, and was long considered an ornament to the town, till eclipsed by more ostentatious structures.

Turning now southwards, the St. Mirren Street of to-day (p. 132), with its garden square on the one side and row of banks and fine shops on the other, is a very different place from what it was fifty years ago. Then it was called the

Water Wynd (p. 133). It was steep, crooked, and narrow; the roadway being only fifteen feet wide and the side walks two feet wide. Yet it was the principal thoroughfare to the southern quarter of the town, and was always a busy place.

Gordon's Loan, 1906.

It could boast of at least three "change houses" on either side, and old Peter Kerr's coffee shop about the middle. This latter was a very primitive place compared with modern restaurants, yet it provided "hamely fare" and comfort by the kitchen fire, where one could have a roll and coffee and a canny smoke. Fun and frolic were not awanting, especially when Jamie, the budding beadle, came with the "wrang waistcoat," and so could not find in the pockets the necessary two-pence, or when big Sandy, the policeman, put the butter in the coffee instead of on his roll.

Those who were otherwise minded could find warm ale and a game at bagatelle at Granny Kerr's. Taddy's snuff

CORNER OF BRIDGE STREET, 1865.

and garden seeds were sold at Stevenson's, and sweeties at Wotherspoon's, at the "Diel's Elbow," at the top of the street (p. 134); while the painter, the printer, the tinsmith, and the chimney sweep could all be found in this important little lane. At the bottom Causeyside opened up, with its shawl warehouses, and the Bank of Scotland at the corner, built on the site of the Old Turf Inn (p. 115).

The buildings in the lower part of Causeyside have not been much altered during the last fifty years, but some old people can still remember the time when many of them were thatched cottages. Although little changed in outward aspect, they are not now tenanted by the same class of people, as they were

Corner of Bridge Street, 1906.
The Author searching for the site of his birth-place.

half a century ago. We no longer see the well dressed-salesmen standing on the steps of the shawl warehouses on the look out for buyers. The corner of Forbes Street was the centre of trade here, and we produce a view of a characteristic old Paisley building which then occupied that angle, where now the offices of the *Paisley Daily Express* are situated (p. 135). This photograph has the further interest in that it includes a lady who has since distinguished herself in philanthropic and Christian work with an energy and success which have endeared her to a large circle of friends.

CAUSEYSIDE STREET, 1892 (CORNER OF GORDON'S LOAN).

A little further up, the transformation of the street on the east side has been very great. At the corner of Orchard Street stood the well-known Peter Robertson's public-house (p. 120), where so many genial souls were accustomed to meet at mid-day for a crack and a dram, and where buyers of a like inclination were entertained. Mention of this classic spot recalls a little incident. When the writer of these lines returned to his native town after many years of absence, he chanced to meet, just at "Peter's" door, an old friend, a retired shawl manufacturer, whom he had not seen for many years. But such friendships made in early days are renewed without ceremony, as if the

CAUSEYSIDE STREET, 1906.

previous meeting had only been yesterday. After the usual greetings, the first thing that the manufacturer said, in a far-away voice, for he was a trifle dull of hearing, was "Are ye dry?" This query made at the door of "Peter's" was rather astonishing. In the old days it would have meant an adjournment inside. But times had changed, and that was impossible. Could it be that the manufacturer had taken to —— ? But that was equally impossible. Nevertheless the circumstances were suspicious. But the mystery was cleared up by the next words, "Can you keep the water out of your windows in stormy weather up at Thornly Park, for we cannot keep it out at the

Canal Bank, 1882.

Brodie?" Thus the last chance of being treated at "Peter's" was gone. It would have been an interesting and unique experience, as the writer, not being a shawl buyer, had never been invited into this renowned "howff."

From this point southwards the erstwhile switch-backed Causeyside has been transformed into a wide street, which only requires trees to make it a handsome boulevard. For this improvement we are largely indebted to the energy of Provost Robert K. Bell (p. 144). The east side has been entirely rebuilt and set back. The section between Causeyside and the Bladda, including "Gordon's Loan and Prussia Street and

SITE OF CANAL BANK, 1906.

Plunken at the end o't," has been completely revolutionized. No other part of the town presents such a scene of destruction. Literally not one stone has been left upon another (pp. 138-139). The line of the streets can no longer be traced, and Gordon's Loan (now Gordon Street) does not now resemble a good shinty, "lying to the lick finely," as in old days. Yet this quarter has been immortalized by the delightful pen of the late David Gilmour, in *Gordon's Loan, Sixty Odd Years Ago*. The present writer feels a satisfaction that he can claim to belong to this classic locality. His parents took up house in the Loan, on their marriage in 1823, and always resided in the neighbourhood, so that his earliest recollections are connected with this part of the town. He even can remember

Robert K. Bell, Provost 1902-5.

the "Coal Ree Parliament" so graphically described by David Gilmour, and knew some members of it, especially Peter Callender. But by this time Peter had long ceased to be an advocate of the equal division of all property and means of production, and was a quiet elderly man who kept a humble school in Marshall's Lane. He was the very image of the schoolmaster in Goldsmith's "Deserted Village."

> "A man severe he was, and stern to view;
> Yet he was kind, or if severe in aught,
> The love he bore to learning was in fault."

Memory still lingers over the low-roofed school-room, which had been a six-loom shop, with its close atmosphere, and abundant and varied smells, where Peter initiated us into the mysteries of the multiplication table and the Shorter Catechism.

Crookston Castle.

Peter was a Unitarian, but out of deference to the popular opinions he, like, Burns, "tairged us tightly" in the "Questions," and got the ministers to inspect the school at times. There was only one boy whose parents objected to this religious instruction, and when we stood up to repeat our "answers," he was simply passed over. He was rather envied by the other boys, especially when the question was, "What is effectual calling?" As is well known, this is one of the most difficult in the book, and unless you got a good start and were not interrupted, there was small chance of getting to the end of it. As for understanding what it was all about, that was quite another matter. Peter was a wise man, and did not venture

CARRIAGEHILL, 1880.

beyond his depth, but contented himself with teaching the Catechism in the orthodox way "without note or comment."

Opinions will differ, no doubt, as to the value of religious teaching in the school, but if we are to judge by results, we must admit that many of Peter's pupils did not turn out badly in after life, although nourished on a diet of "Calvinism and a little oatmeal."

On the last day of school, before the Saint James' Day Fair Holidays, we all appeared in clean "dadlies" to pay our modest —very modest—fees. There were no lessons that day, but the master sat at his table and called us up one by one, receipted

CARRIAGEHILL, 1906.

the little bill with a flourish, for he was a fine penman, and handed each of us a new penny from a bag on the desk. But there were always some whom he did not call up. These were too poor, or had guardians too unthrifty to be ready with the money. But kindly Peter would not punish the children for the shortcomings of their parents, so he went round the circle and gave each of these unfortunates a penny like the rest of us,

and then we were joyfully dismissed to spend our wealth at the
"shows." This quaint old quarter is now entirely swept away.
The author, when searching for the site of his birth-place, No. 1
Bridge Street of the old time, could only make out that it was
now somewhere in the middle of the street (p. 139).

LINN AT GLENFIELD.

Southwards from Gordon's Loan, the east side of Causeyside
has been entirely rebuilt (p. 140). It contained the Tea Gardens,
and many old houses with outside stairs. The street was steep
then, but now the gradient has been much improved (p. 141).
The Canal Railway crosses near the top of the brae. In the
days of old Paisley the path by the banks of the canal was a
favourite walk. Here the shawl designers were wont to take

their mid-day "dauner" to stretch their legs and ease their fingers. These men formed a considerable element in the weaving trade of that time, and anyone who will take the trouble of looking over the design and pattern books, a goodly number of which

TANNAHILL CONCERT.

are now happily preserved in the Museum, will be astonished no less at the beauty than at the extreme microscopical minuteness of detail in their works. Such charming designs could only be worked out by men of considerable culture and refined taste. Every day about noon they ceased their labours for a short period of repose. The accessibility and beauty of the canal bank (p. 142) made it a desirable place for their rambles. The walk, which was lovely all the way, usually extended to Hawkhead, passing the "gley't brig" at Blackhall, that marvel of architecture, the stability of which the boys could never understand. The frequent passage of the "fly boats," which were drawn by horses,

SITE OF DUNN SQUARE, 1890.

and went at a good pace, made the scene lively, and the scarlet coats of the riders gave colour to the picture. On Saturdays the walk might be prolonged to Crookston Castle (p. 145), a ruin perched on a knoll amidst exquisite woodland scenery, and associated, like many more of the castles and yew trees of our country, with the memory of the hapless and beautiful Mary

Queen of Scots. This walk is well described by Alexander Smith, himself at one time a pattern designer, in his story of "Alfred Haggart's Household."

The presence in Paisley of these designers was a decided advantage to the artistic and literary society of the town. That

DUNN SQUARE, LOOKING WEST, 1906.

eminent artist, Sir J. Noel Paton, was one of them; and the New Paisley may well regret the loss of a class of men so cultured. The leading industries of the town, although excellent in their own way, do not now require the same artistic services.

Continuing our ramble southwards, we pass through Charleston, a noted suburb in the days of the shawl trade. It also has undergone great changes. A few of the one-storey thatched houses still linger, and more of the two-storey lands about Carriagehill (p. 146-7); but the streets are constantly being widened, and most of these relics of the past have disappeared, giving

Dunn Square, looking East, 1906.

more space for the ever increasing traffic, and the advent of the electric cars. Beyond Carriagehill we come to Colinslee. This was the principal seat of the block printing of shawls, which flourished as the harness weaving fell away. These printers, who earned good wages for a time, were rather "swells" in their way, and kept up a brass band for the entertainment of the district. Just as the harness weaver had a draw-boy, each block printer had a "tearer." These tearers were boys and girls, and if the draw-boys were a demonstrative class, the tearers were not behind them. When the day's work was over, they issued in a stream from the gate, with their hands and arms stained with all the colours of the rainbow, and made the streets lively on the way home. Block printing was also carried on extensively at the north end of the town, at Arkleston and Nethercommon; and in the Museum are to be seen many beautiful specimens of the delicate work which was there produced.

The electric cars now carry us further out, so that shortly we may find ourselves in the beautiful grounds of Glenfield, admiring the lovely waterfall of "The Linn" (p. 148), or listening to the sweet strains at the Tannahill Concert. This annual gathering, by the kindness of the laird of the Glen, is held in a natural amphitheatre on the slope of Gleniffer Braes. Here the songs of Tannahill and others are sung to the delight of large gatherings (p. 149). The proceeds were first devoted to erecting a statue to Tannahill, and afterwards one to Burns. Since then the money has been devoted to the Royal Alexandra Infirmary. The sum frequently amounts to nearly £300 each year, and should this be continued, as seems probable, the time may come when poor Tannahill, who never had £300 in his life, may have become as large a contributor to this excellent institution as any of its wealthy supporters.

We now return to the Cross. The view of the Clark Halls was obstructed by a mass of unimportant buildings which filled the angle at the top of Saint Mirren Street (p. 150). The Town Council resolved to remove these, but found this a difficult task, made more difficult and expensive by frequent changes of plan, till Sir William Dunn came to the rescue, and to his generosity we owe the completion of this great improvement (p. 152).

SITE OF GEORGE A. CLARK HALLS, 1865.

Sir William Dunn, like William Barbour and many others, was "evicted" from Paisley by the decay of the shawl trade. Not finding scope for his energies in a declining industry, he pushed his way in the African trade, and ultimately became a wealthy London merchant. He showed his love for the town by numerous handsome benefactions, and represented it in Parliament for fourteen years.

The Dunn Square, with the statues of Her Majesty the late Queen Victoria, and of the two brothers, Sir Peter and Mr. Thomas Coats, opening up as it does a fine view of the beautiful Clark Town Halls (p. 152), is one of the most successful

GEORGE A. CLARK HALLS, 1906.

efforts yet made for the reconstruction and adornment of the town.

The only building in the block so removed which memory lingers upon, is the Artizans' Institution, founded in 1847, which stood at the south-west corner of the bridge (p. 95). This was a centre of much beneficent influence on education in Paisley. Mr. Thomas Coats, whose statue now appropriately stands on this site (p. 151), was a warm supporter, and many gentlemen of cultivated tastes and enlightened ideas, among whom may be mentioned Dr. W. B. M'Kinlay, James J. Lamb, and Thomas MacRobert, were at various times connected with it. The

ABBEY BEFORE RESTORATIONS, 1835.

Literary Union of the Artizans' Institution drew together many remarkable men in their humble way. John Shaw, John Broom, and James Lindsay, were men who, under more favourable circumstances, might have made some noise in the world.

The old bridge has been widened since those days, and is now named Saint James' Bridge. This saint seems to have been popular in Paisley, for amongst the thread people the name of James occurs with embarrassing frequency.

WEST FRONT OF ABBEY, WITH METHODIST CHAPEL, 1858.

Up to 1860, the Abbey Close was an unsavoury locality. In English towns the Cathedral Close, which usually conducts to the west front of the Cathedral or Abbey, is invariably a quiet, sleepy street of old-fashioned houses, with bow windows, hid in creepers, and everything exceptionally clean and neat. Such, probably, was our Abbey Close in early times, and doubtless in this quarter the hamlet of Paisley first began. But in the days of

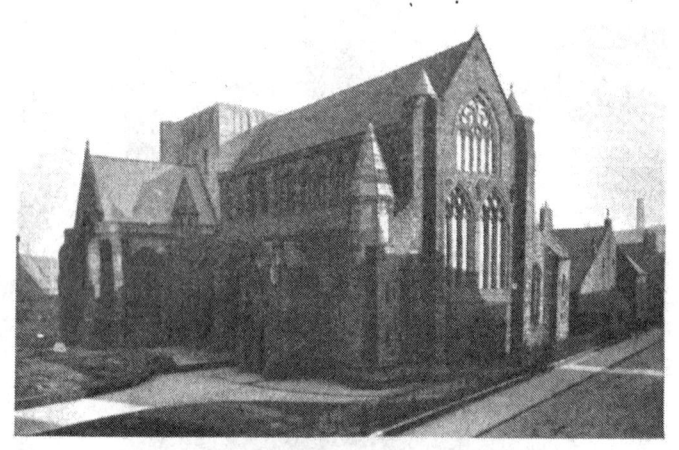

Abbey with Restorations, 1904.

which we are speaking, the Close was never other than a sort of Paddy's Market, of tumble-down second-hand shops. It appeared to rain there more frequently than in any other part of the town, for we never recollect the wretchedly uneven street being without ample pools of water.

None of these buildings were of architectural or historic value, and the clearing of them away, and the erection of the magnificent Clark Town Halls was one of the greatest improvements ever made in Paisley (p. 152). It brought into view

THE PLACE OF PAISLEY, 1865.

the fine proportions of the Abbey. This beautiful building (pp. 156-7-8), has been partially restored in recent years, and is well deserving of further restoration. In Scotland we never had so many of those rich ecclesiastical establishments as they have in England, and in the troublous and destructive times of our Reformation, many of them were mutilated or destroyed. But the beauty of Gothic architecture is now much more generally

CROSS, LOOKING WEST, 1905.

appreciated, and the desire is strong to preserve the few good specimens that we yet possess. The Abbey of Paisley is one of the finest of these old churches. The west front is a composition of exceeding purity and grace, and many of the internal features are equally fine. Surely some one of the public-spirited and wealthy sons of Paisley will do honour to his native place and himself by restoring the Abbey to its pristine beauty. Of the secular buildings which must have clustered around the Abbey, we give, under the name of the "Place of Paisley," the only portion now remaining (p. 159). This house was at one time occupied by the Duke of Abercorn, and later by Lord Dundonald.

HIGH STREET, LOOKING EAST, 1879.

From the Abbey Bridge, formerly known as the Seedhills Bridge, a fine view can be obtained of the Hammills, over which, when in flood, the river pours with a roar which can be heard at a considerable distance (p. 25). In summer days the pool at the Hammills was much frequented by bathers, and it was considered a great feat when a boy could "tail the Linn," that is, swim across this pool. The presence of this reef of rocks probably decided the position selected for the Abbey. The linn supplied fish for the Friday's dinner, and the fall was used, as it still is, to drive a meal mill, for the monks of those days were great civilizers. Nearly every Abbey in the kingdom is built on a spot such as this, and probably for the same reasons.

Coming back to the Cross, we turn our steps westward, and again are confronted with extensive changes. The steeple is gone, and so the Cross is deprived of its greatest ornament. The north side of High Street as far as Churchhill has been all cleared away, and the building line set back (p. 160). Before this was done, High Street was a narrow thoroughfare (p. 161), crowded on Saturday nights, when "Daunie Weir," a Paisley "character," perambulated it selling ballads, among which was Alexander Wilson's "Watty and Meg," and reciting the popular poem in a husky voice. Paisley boys could all repeat "Watty and Meg," although few of them had seen it in print. They learned it from "Daunie" (p. 163).

Of the old houses removed up to 1882, when High Street was widened, the most remarkable was the town house of the Sempills, with the family arms sculptured on the front. This stone is now preserved in the Museum. The first Lord Sempill fell along with his King on the fatal field of Flodden, so that he was one of those "Flowers o' the Forest" that were "a' wede away."

Near to the Rob Roy Close, which led up to School Wynd, was Thomas Goodlet's "Coffee House," the proprietor of which had a reputation for comic song and story, all his own, and was consequently in great demand for social gatherings. This place was also a favourite resort of the aspiring youths of the Literary Union of the Artizan's Institution before mentioned. Here over their coffee many "Noctes Ambrosianae" were spent,

"DAUNIE" WEIR.

which linger in the memory of not a few survivors, most of whom, characteristically, are members of the Philosophical Institution. William Peattie, Robert Russell, James Hay, and others, have done no discredit to the training obtained at the Literary Union.

The corner of New Street shows a characteristic old building, and its rather fantastic successor (pp. 164-5); but soon this angle will be occupied by a handsome building for the Young Men's Christian Association. By the kindness of the architect, Mr. T. Graham Abercrombie, who has done much to ornament the town, we are enabled to give an elevation of the proposed structure

Corner of New Street, 1902.

(p. 166). The next block to the south in New Street was the well-known shop of George Caldwell, printer and bookseller. George was blessed with a rather eccentric wife, who always went among the young people by the name of "Lady" Caldwell. She was an enthusiastic temperance reformer, and resided at the Teetotal Tower in Renfrew Road. This was a great resort of the youngsters, and boasted of a camera obscura (p. 167).

Visitors mounted a wooden stair to a dark room, and made a circle round a table covered with a white cloth, when by a movement of the lenses there was shown a picture of the surrounding country with carts driving, and men ploughing the

Corner of New Street, 1905.

fields with horses an inch in height, a moving living wonder. "Lady Caldwell" would treat them to a lecture, and Geordie, her husband, would play the fiddle to those who cared to indulge in a "penny reel." These were economical days, when the extravagance of a Fancy Ball was not dreamed of.

Turning to the north at New Street, we notice the spire of the High Church, erected in 1754 (p. 197), which occupies a commanding position, and has long been admired for its graceful and well-balanced proportions. Close to it on the right is the old Grammar School, round which linger many pleasant memories of past days; and delightful recollections of dear

PROPOSED BUILDING FOR YOUNG MEN'S CHRISTIAN ASSOCIATION.

old Dr. Brunton, than whom no Paisley teacher was ever more respected. Further on, at No. 82, stood the "Wee Steeple," the bell of which was tolled for every passing funeral procession. The building was demolished in 1807, and the bell removed to the gatehouse of Hope Temple Gardens. A narrow passage by the side of the "Wee Steeple" was called the "Pen Brae," and led up to Oakshaw Street, before Orr Square was formed. It was in a building, still existing, in this lane that the " Pen Folk" met, who have been immortalized by the late David Gilmour.

Further westwards and nearly opposite the Museum, stood the house in which Professor John Wilson ("Christopher North")

TEETOTAL TOWER, 1860.

was born. This was an extremely interesting old building. On entering, you stood in the kitchen, with its stone floor and roomy baronial fire-place. Passing in to the adjoining room, the eye wandered from the old mantle-shelf, with the figures of a shepherd and his dog and flock, ornamenting its centre, to the quaintly panelled doors and wainscotted walls. Climbing the richly carved, oaken-railed staircase, you reached the dining-room, with its figured cornice rising from antique dados and panels. In a room near by, one observed the elaborate mouldings around the bed with folding doors, where "wee Kit" first saw the light. We give a view of the building in its later days, when it contained the shop of "Teugh Geordie," a noted confectioner, who was a special favourite of the young people. On the building which replaces this interesting old house, a tablet has been placed, of which we give a reproduction (p. 169). The north

BIRTHPLACE OF PROFESSOR JOHN WILSON, 1894.

side of the street at this point contains the Free Library and Museum, the Drill Hall, and the Coats Memorial Church, three of the great ornaments of the "New Paisley."

Proceeding westwards, we arrive at the separation of Sandholes, popularly known as the "Coffin En'" (pp. 176-7). This is the "Cross" of the West-end. Beyond this point further widenings are in progress, and although now the "bonnie woods o' Craigielea," where

"The cushat croodles amorously,"

and even "sweet Ferguslie," have long been folded in the embrace of the advancing town, the electric cars now take us out quickly to where,

"Towering o'er the Newton woods,
Lav'rocks fan the snaw-white clouds."

TABLET TO PROFESSOR WILSON, 1906.

We can thence continue our walk by the "Dusky Glen" and other familiar haunts of Tannahill, where still the sweet wild flowers bloom and the birds sing, which delighted him so much;

and so by "Stanley green shaw" (p. 171), we can climb Gleniffer. Here we may pause by

"The bonnie wee well on the breist o' the brae,"

which Hugh Macdonald, himself at one time a Colinslee block printer, has rendered classic, and, looking back, we will behold one of the fairest prospects in the country.

HUGH MACDONALD'S "WEE WELL."

Probably it was from this spot that the advancing Roman legions, keeping to the heights, as was their habit, first had unfolded before them the kingdom of Strath-Clyde. There it lay, stretching far and wide, and, on the north-west horizon, they could descry, in the blue distance, the mighty rampart of the Grampians, little dreaming that beyond this barrier imperial Rome should never penetrate. We may suppose the centurion halting his troops to refresh themselves at this well, before descending to pitch their tents on the last of those glacial rolls which, like waves of the sea, fill up the space between the base of the hills and the morass which then occupied the low lands. It was on the summit of Oakshaw Hill that the Prætorium, or gate next the enemy, was pitched, and Castlehead still marks the other extremity of the camp.

STANLEY CASTLE.

The view of Paisley from this point is very fine, and the Corporation are to be congratulated on having secured a considerable area for a public park. They have wisely left it in its native state, to the delight of all lovers of the picturesque. The rambler can then go on to the renowned Peesweep Inn (p. 172), on the summit of the hill, where he can be regaled with the Spartan fare of bread and cheese and ginger beer, for our maternal magistracy believe that the sweet mountain air is intoxicating enough for the present degenerate race! Then, as gloaming comes on, he can return to see that

"The plantin taps are tinged with goud,"

and in the hollow,

"The midges dance aboon the burn."

PEESWEEP INN.

Every turn of the road recalls Paisley's sweet singer. At the Half-timers' School at Ferguslie, we may rest for a moment, and, looking through the railing, we will see a section of the old canal. There is the narrow towing path (p. 173) and the quaint little bridge, and near it the culvert which carried the Maxwellton burn underneath the canal. The rivulet and the canal being nearly upon a level, a tunnel of masonry had to be constructed in the form of a syphon, to carry the stream to the other side of the canal. This necessitated a deep pit, or pool, on each side, which, of course, was always full of water, up to the level of the stream on each side. These holes, as can still be seen, were surrounded by a low wall, but had no other protection. Here, in the early morning of 17th May, 1810, " Black Peter,"* a well-known negro weaver, brought up the lifeless body of poor Tannahill. We must drop a tear of pity for the hapless fate of one who carried through the world the "white flower of a blameless life," alas! too early

TANNAHILL'S HOLE.

blighted, but made beautiful by song, and remember with gratitude the considerateness of Messrs. Coats in preserving this pathetic memorial of a sad event.

Then in crossing George Street we may note in the centre of the causeway the horse-shoe which marks the spot where was enacted the deplorable tragedy of the burning for witchcraft,

---

* There is a biography of Peter Burnet ("Black Peter") in the Free Public Library.

with which the name of Christian Shaw, the originator of the thread trade, was mixed up. We may then return by Castle Street, where Tannahill was born, or by Queen Street, where he lived (p. 175). The former building no longer exists, but the latter still remains, and in connection with it we may here preserve an interesting reminiscence. The following statement was made, in 1898, by George Archibald, a weaver

TANNAHILL'S BIRTHPLACE IN CASTLE STREET.

who occupied the same house and worked at the same loom, that had been used by Tannahill, and is kindly given to us by his sons, Messrs. George and Robert Archibald, manufacturers in Paisley. George Archibald, Senr., says:—

"I have pleasure in sending you a few notes which are in my own recollection correct. This happened about the year 1835, sixty-three years ago. I was at that time weaving in No. 6 Queen Street, on the same exact loomstead as our poet Robert Tannahill used to weave on.

"This loomstead was situated on the south side of the property; its exact position was at the south-east corner next the fire, the window looking eastward. This loomstead, to suit the light from the window, was put up as what is known in the trade as a left-hand loom. I would weave on this loomstead for about six years, and in this way my back was to the wall,

TANNAHILL'S HOUSE, NO. 6 QUEEN STREET.

and a small recess in the gable, which was said to be often used by the poet, as a place where he kept his books and papers. When anything new struck him, all he had to do was to turn round to this recess, and note it down, while on his loom.

"It was always remarked that he was very charitable, as he had generally a sixpence or a shilling on the top of his loom to spare to any deserving person or charitable object. I was often called upon while working on this loomstead by visitors, and had pleasure in pointing out these small particulars to any who called.

"Amongst the visitors was an old lady and her son, whom she called 'Wull' (William, I presume). She came from Old Kilpatrick once a year for many years. My father, John Archibald, was weaving in the same shop, and 'Wull' would ask him liberty for his mother to get a few minutes to give vent to her

THE "COFFIN EN'," 1885.

feelings, on the exact spot on which our poet used to sit. I was asked to come off my loom, and allow her a few minutes of meditation. She would always shed a few tears, as my cloth was always a little wet when she left. I remember this as well as if it were yesterday; she would often pick up my 'pooking pin,' and grasp the lay, giving expression to the following, 'Robin, Robin, whar is ta noo?' She would repeat this two or three times, finishing up with, 'My dear Robin, whar is ta noo?' Her name I do not remember; the above I remember well, as she always left a sixpence for me, which was a very important part of the proceedings to me at that time.

"Before leaving the property, she would always go down the garden to view the 'Lily-Oak' tree that the poet had planted.

"Among many other remarks that were often made in this loom-shop, was one by our poet's brother, James Tannahill, who was proprietor of this property, No. 6 Queen Street, which is also

The "Coffin En'," 1905.

quite fresh in my memory; this was on the night before his fatal end. A county gentleman gave a supper and ball in what we now know as the Abercorn Rooms, a hotel at that time. Amongst the guests invited was our poet, and other literary men of the day. During the ball Tannahill and another friend were crossing the room, when our poet heard a remark by a visitor speaking to a friend, 'Who was that little man?' and the reply given was, 'That was the poet Tannahill.' 'What a diminutive creature.' This remark is said to have made him very sad that night, as at this time our poet's mind was said to be a little unhinged. Tannahill is said to have gone home all right that morning to his widowed mother, and his little pet dog. Our poet's mother was disturbed by this dog barking in the morning; she rose to see what was the matter, she examined the house, but her son Robin was absent, and in the later part of the morning she told some of the neighbours about this; so my father, John Archibald, along with five other neighbours, all weavers, arranged to go in search of Tannahill. They agreed to go in pairs, and try to find him out. My father and John Fletcher were to search the woods of Craigielea; the other pair, James Laird and a darkey known as Black Peter Burnet, were to search Gleniffer Braes; and the last pair, to search Hawkhead district, their names I cannot remember at present. The pair composed of Black Peter and James Laird were passing the fatal spot, when Black Peter observed a cap and a scarf on the ridge that surrounds what is now known as 'Tannahill's Hole.' It is often said that Black Peter dived down in search of Tannahill, but this is not correct, as the writer of these notes knew Black Peter intimately. He was a regular visitor to my father's house twenty-six years after the sad event, and Black Peter's remarks were that his fellow-searcher, James Laird, procured a set of what is called 'creepers' from a small house then (now removed) on the opposite side of the Canal. They searched with these creepers, and Black Peter Burnet was the one that found the body of our poet Tannahill with these creepers. For this act this same Black Peter Burnet received from our poet's brother, James Tannahill, a free house and loomstead till he died."

We make no apology for introducing here for preservation this quaint narrative, for all matters, however trivial, which concern Tannahill, are dear to every Paisley man.

Mr. William Brown.

In concluding this review of the transition period between the Old and New Paisley, we call attention to an interesting group, taken at the instance of the late Mr. John Polson, in 1882, on the "Last Canal Boat," immediately before the canal was replaced by the railway. It contains portraits of a number of well-known townsmen of that time, and was taken by Mr. William Brown, photographic artist, Gilmour Street, by whose kindness we are enabled to reproduce it.

The Last Canal Boat, 1882.

KEY TO "THE LAST CANAL BOAT."

Photograph taken by Mr. William Brown, at Canal Basin, 27th May, 1882.

NAMES BEGINNING AT LEFT.

Front Row.

1. A. S. SKINNIDER, reporter.
2. JAMES ALCORN, Agent of Canal.
3. JAMES BARCLAY, Canal Bank.
4. WM. A. LOCHHEAD, *Paisley Daily Express.*
5. CHARLES DAVIDSON, architect.
6. JOHN POLSON.
7. ALEX. GARDNER, publisher.
8. ROBERT ROBERTSON, waiter (at the further end).

Second Row.

9. WILLIAM POLSON.
10. Bailie ALEX. SPEIRS.
11. JAMES FINLAYSON, Director of G. & S.-W. Railway Co.
12. Provost WILLIAM MACKEAN.
13. JAMES CLARK, Chapel House, afterwards Provost.
14. Bailie JAMES WILLS.
15. JOHN JOHNSTON, afterwards Provost.

Third Row.

16. PETER WALLACE, Councillor, First Ward.
17. Bailie EAGLESIM (hat only seen).
18. Bailie JOHN YOUNG, wood merchant.

Third Row.

19. WM. B. BARBOUR, M.P.
20. Rev. A. G. FLEMING.
21. Dr. RICHMOND.
22. DAVID GILMOUR of *The Pen Folk.*

Fourth Row.

23. NORMAN M. MACKEAN.
24. Provost SHANKS of Johnstone.
25. WM. ABERCROMBIE, Union Bank.
26. JAMES A. MACKEAN.
27. WILLIAM BOW.
28. WM. FINLATOR, Royal Bank.
29. JOHN BARTLEMORE (half face).
30. P. C. MACGREGOR of Brediland.
31. JAMES DREWETTE, *Glasgow Daily Mail.*
32. JAMES CALDWELL, County Clerk.
33. Major FULLARTON.

Back Row.

34. MATTHEW BLAIR, clothier.
35. ROBERT RICHARDSON, Gateside.
36. ROBERT SHARP, Master of Works.

Present, but not distinctly seen, DAVID YOUNG, Town Clerk, behind Bailie Wills; and G. R. MACKENZIE, purveyor, in saloon, at stern.

CHAPTER XII

NEW PAISLEY

WITH whatever sentimental feelings we may linger over the picture of Old Paisley, we by no means wish to undervalue the vast advantages of a material kind which the New Paisley presents. The old order changes, giving place to new, and, in general, to better conditions. Mechanical inventions have placed conveniences and even luxuries within the reach of the humblest, such as were never dreamed of in the so-called "good old times." Everything depends upon a proper use being made of these benefits, and while some, no doubt, abuse them, these are a minority, and the people as a rule have made great advances.

The expansion of the town since the shawl trade decayed has been considerable. The population of Paisley was in

1875, - - 51,209		
1885, - - 59,108	Increase,	7,899
1895, - - 71,622	,,	12,514
1905, - - 85,604	,,	13,982
Increase in 30 years, - -		34,395

This remarkable increase is largely due to immigration, which naturally has had a considerable influence on the character of the people. The incomers have brought many new ideas and practices, which have materially changed the homely style of life that previously existed. We would, however, fain hope

DAVID WILSON, PROVOST, 1900-2.

that their advent, while widening the views, has also improved the character of the population. It is to be feared, however, that the industries which have created the New Paisley, have not preserved that artistic taste and culture which marked the epoch of handicraft work. They do not lend themselves to artistic treatment or study, and this defect may have to be remedied in some other way.

The increase in the assessable rental has been correspondingly great.

VALUATION OF THE BURGH OF PAISLEY.

Year	
1857-58,	£99,628
1859-60,	101,952
1869-70,	126,185
1879-80,	203,329
1889-90,	268,176
1899-1900,	340,185
1905-06,	402,337
1906-07,	410,187

The rental has thus quadrupled in fifty years.

One of the best evidences of the improved condition of the New Paisley, is to be found in the details of the death-rate. In 1875, Paisley held an unenviable position among the eight principal towns of Scotland. This unfortunate state of affairs was not unnoticed by the Town Council, and efforts were made to improve it, but it was not till 1886 that a department for Public Health, Cleansing, and Drainage was formed, and the matter taken seriously in hand. Ashpits were condemned, drainage districts were formed, and the whole system of refuse collection and destruction was placed on an improved footing. An important step was the adoption, in 1891, of the Compulsory Notification of Infectious Diseases Act, and since then the health of the town has been carefully supervised.

The following table shows how marked and continuous has been the decline in the death-rate in recent years.

DEATH-RATE PER 1,000 OF THE POPULATION IN PAISLEY.

Average of five years ending	1875,	-	29·08
,,	,,	1880,	-	26·66
,,	,,	1885,	-	24·72
,,	,,	1890,	-	23·48
,,	,,	1895,	-	21·34
,,	,,	1900,	-	19·86
,,	,,	1905,	-	17·96

while, if 1905 be taken by itself, it amounted only to 16·1.

Between 1875 and 1905, this gives a saving of 11·12 per 1,000, which, calculated on a population of 85,000, amounts to 945 lives per annum. No doubt this reduction was partly due to other causes than improved sanitation, but the labours of the Public Health Committee have largely contributed to this satisfactory result. In this connection the public cannot forget the eminent services of Provost David Wilson (p. 183), who, for the fourteen years from 1886 to 1900, was Convener of that Committee, and was unwearied in his exertions to improve the health of the town.

Previous to 1838, Paisley was supplied with water from pump wells, with the result that infectious diseases, and especially fever, were very prevalent, and the dreaded cholera made occasional visits. In that year the water from Stanley was introduced, mainly by the exertions of Dr. James Kerr. But the town outgrew this supply, and the Rowbank scheme was added. Even this soon became inadequate for the rapidly increasing population, and the Council had to cross the valley from the Gleniffer range, and tap the streams on the Kilbirnie hills in the Rye scheme in 1883; so that now the population of Paisley and some of the neighbouring parts possess an ample supply of this most necessary element. The carrying out of the Rye scheme was largely due to the exertions of Provost William MacKean (p. 187).

The drainage of Paisley, which at one time was very bad, has been continuously improved since 1879, and may now be considered satisfactory. Damp and unwholesome houses, however picturesque, have been replaced by dwellings constructed with the latest sanitary improvements. The purification of the atmosphere from smoke, however, yet leaves much to be desired, and the state of the River Cart, both as to cleanliness and utility as a means of traffic, calls for attention.

The widening of the streets has also been going on for many years. The growing traffic of an ever increasing population demanded this convenience, and the greater air space and light thus obtained have had excellent effects on the health of the community. This improvement in the appearance of the town has been largely due to the perseverance of Provosts Murray, MacKean, and Bell, and the work is still being prosecuted.

The public buildings in Paisley supply excellent evidence

of the general improvement of taste in architecture which has been going on. Many of the churches have been rebuilt or rearranged, and some are handsome structures. The Clark Halls, the Free Public Library and Museum, the Drill Hall, the Coats Memorial Church, the John Neilson Institution, the

William MacKean, Provost, 1879-82.

New Grammar School, the Technical College, the Sheriff Court House, the New County Buildings, and the Royal Alexandra Infirmary, are edifices of which any town might be proud. The Royal Victoria Eye Infirmary, built, equipped, and gifted by Provost Archibald Mackenzie (p. 195), is also a tasteful building. The mill property has in many cases been erected on artistic lines, and the street vistas now everywhere are much improved.

The laudable desire to reside in the country is strong, and neat, and in many cases handsome villas are springing up in all the suburbs. The convenience of the electric cars largely contributes to this spreading of the population, and is one of the many beneficial and happy results of science that this generation has seen.

The educational advantages also of the New Paisley are far in advance of the Old. Time was when the only passable academy in the town was the Grammar School, taught by Dr. Brunton, who was a capable and much admired teacher. Even this consisted of only one room, where all the classes met together, and none of the other schools in the town had any better accommodation. Female education was frequently relegated to a few genteel old ladies of limited acquirements. Now, there are excellent means of instruction for all classes. The Board Schools are large and finely equipped, and an admirably organised Technical College and School of Art provides a class of training which was never dreamed of in the past. In the Free Public Library an abundant supply of the best literature of the day and of past times, is at the command of every person, so that the fountains of knowledge are many, and freely open to all.

But more particularly does the marked absence of signs of poverty strike the observer, and all the more forcibly if he is old enough to remember what Paisley was in the latter part of the weaving days. Thanks to the varied industries which have replaced the shawl trade, to the enterprise of the people, and to the cheapness of necessary comforts which our new industrial system has produced, the frequent recurring depressions and consequent misery of former times, no longer afflict Paisley. Those who are willing to do well, find ample employment. The feeble and the really unfortunate are assisted by numerous

JOHN NEILSON INSTITUTION.

benevolent agencies, so that where poverty exists, the causes can generally be traced to misconduct.

The contrast between the Old and the New Paisley, is nowhere more strongly illustrated than among the young people. In the weaving days the draw-boys were conspicuous. They were a rough-and-tumble lot, rude of manners, abundant in tatters, and rank socialists, every one of them, for they believed in the equal division of all wealth, especially the fruits of the earth, which they always held to be public property. The girls of those days were hardly thought of at all. But now in the times of the Paisley thread, the girls monopolize attention. To describe all their excellences would be impossible. As Burns recoiled from a similar task in "Tam o' Shanter"—

"Sic flights are far beyond our pow'r."

To make fun of them is a dangerous proceeding. Their resentment is not to be lightly incurred. If they could hustle an obnoxious lady agitator, or besiege a mill manager, what would they not do to a "mere man" who failed to render justice to their merits? Woe to such a critic should he encounter them at the corner of Maxwellton Street or the Bladda, at two or six o'clock, when the mills were "skailing"! To say, in West End parlance, that "they are a bardy set," might be true, but it is only the Paisley way of saying that, like other Scotch folks, they "have a guid conceit of themselves."

Yet the study of the crowd which issues from the mills (pp. 198-9) is a great revelation, especially to anyone who can remember a similar scene fifty years ago. Gone are all the shoeless feet, the jupe and the petticoat, the tartan shawl over the head, and the subdued air of hard times. Now there is a rush of young and hopeful life, jubilant that the day's confinement is over, and loud in conversation on how to spend the evening's freedom. Neat and comfortable in attire, with frequent touches of art and taste in dress. No tatters, as in the draw-boy days, no work of unhandy dressmakers, but smart costumes of harmonious colours, and warm woollen "tammies," natty sailor hats, or fashionable motor "scones" to cover the head.

And these girls are not without public spirit and enterprise. We have seen what they did for the Infirmary Bazaar, and

New Grammar School.

during the South African War they busied themselves knitting for the soldiers. In most cases the articles bore the name of the knitter, and, could we know all, there might be many a romantic story and, perhaps, sequel to these gifts. The soldiers on the veldt who opened these welcome parcels, and found that Maggie and Jeanie at home in the mills had been thinking of them, and had been anxious for their comfort, will not soon forget the Paisley thread girls.

But agreeable to the eye as is the crowd of neatly dressed girls as they issue from the mill gates, it is nothing to the appearance of these same young ladies on a holiday or a Sunday. Then they come out in their splendour. " Even Solomon in all his glory was not arrayed like one of these." A susceptible Italian visitor, in 1788, wrote in the *Weaver's Magazine*, that " Paisley abounded in beautiful women, who, in the evening, met in groups, dressed with much elegance and taste, and promenaded in the one street which then formed the town, and after the walk almost every evening there was a dance." This promenade of fair ladies still continues, and may be seen any Sunday evening on the Glasgow Road, or any of the main avenues leading into the country (p. 201).

The conditions of life are very much easier now. Many most beautiful textile fabrics have been brought within reach of the humblest. The unfortunate upper classes can no longer retain the exclusive use of any article of adornment. The Paisley girls quickly find it out, or an imitation of it. In vain the costumiers rise early and sit up late, and compass sea and land to find some novelty with which the mill girls cannot compete. They have to give up the effort in despair.

If the draw-boys were socialists, the thread girls are individualists of a pronounced character. They have no idea of having all things in common. They each have an eye on a house of their own, and the not too distant prospect of a drawing-room, with, as a companion, one of those smart young gentlemen in fashionable suits, brown shoes, bowler hats, and cigarettes, on whom they have shot their invincible glances on the Sunday promenade.

Paisley has had much done for it by its liberal sons and daughters. This work concerns itself solely with the Thread Trade, but other branches of industry have also been prosperous

TECHNICAL COLLEGE AND SCHOOL OF ART.

from similar impelling causes; and those Paisley men who have gone forth to seek their fortunes elsewhere have, in frequent cases, returned laden with their sheaves, and have not been slow in bestowing benefits on their native town. To attempt any detail of these generous actions would lead us away from our subject, but they cannot be overlooked in any comparison of Old and New Paisley. The gifts and legacies of Neilson, Wright, Brodie, Brough, Barbour, Dunn, Mackenzie, and many others, show the love which they entertained for the old place.

It may be said of some people that the more you do for them, the less they will do for themselves. A community can be spoiled by too much kindness. Happily, great as have been the benefits conferred upon the New Paisley, there are no signs that they have enervated the people. On the contrary, intellectual activity and business enterprise are conspicuous. They have not lost the stamina of the old weaver population. These old men, our forefathers, had a more limited range of advantages, but they made up for it by a diligent use of what they had. In the old times if anyone required a restful holiday, he was recommended to try "the Largs," a weaving village on the Firth of Clyde about twenty-two miles from Paisley. But as there was no regular conveyance, the invalid was expected to walk the distance, with the remote chance of getting a lift for a mile or two from some farmer's cart. This preliminary exercise was sure to set him up, and it is surprising what grand walkers the weavers were. As they were unable to wander hundreds of miles in search of the beautiful, they turned their patient eyes on the wild flowers that bloomed in loveliness by the road-side; the insects that sported their brief existence in the summer air; and the wild birds which made the woods vocal with their artless melody. There, and in the poetry descriptive of such scenes, they found their enjoyment, and the local Museum is enriched by the collections in Natural History brought together by some of these worthy men. The inhabitants of the New Paisley possess still these privileges and advantages, and many more. That they may use them aright for the honour of the town, is the fervent wish of all who have the good reputation of Paisley sincerely at heart.

Archibald Mackenzie, Provost, 1894-1900.

Much as we may all rejoice in the material prosperity of Paisley, a word of caution may be dropped, "lest we forget."

The superseding of hand labour by mechanical appliances has been the main cause of all this progress. The leaders of industry have brought it about, and have reaped a rich harvest. But what of the working man? No doubt the reward of labour is greater now than it was, and the purchasing power of wages still further benefits the labouring classes. But the system of working in factories, and large workshops, which was an inevitable result of the new organization of industry, has brought influences of a seriously detrimental character upon the worker. The joy of labour and the exercise of taste and skill in handicraft are gone, and replaced by the monotonous drudgery of tending a machine. Year in, year out, the same dull round of uninteresting and unintellectual labour is his lot. And there appears to be no remedy; and one cannot look without pity and almost with despair, at this apparently inevitable result of our magnificent industrial system.

Need we wonder that relief from this oppressive monotony is sought in some violent exercise of the limbs or the mind? The almost brutal game of football attracts its thousands, while the quieter games of cricket and bowls are not nearly so popular; and those delightful and instructive botanical rambles in which the old weavers delighted, are quite despised. Then the mental excitement of betting on horse races is simply a revulsion from the intellectual numbness of the factory employment, although it is well known that this is not a game of skill, and that the odds are calculated so as to be greatly against the bettors. Light and frivolous amusements appear to have great attractions.

Family life also has suffered. The control and training of the rising generation are not what they ought to be. The young people too often mistake rudeness for independence, coarse language for wit, and vulgarity for manliness. From such an upbringing we cannot hope to produce that conscientious and intelligent labour which is still demanded and highly valued, notwithstanding all our mechanical advances, and, indeed, in consequence of them.

High Church and Old Grammar School.

Workmen associate themselves for many purposes of great utility. If they would combine to improve the quality of labour, and so render it more valuable and remunerative to the buyer, it would command a higher price, and we would hear less of unemployment and of labour wars. The country which possesses the most reliable class of labour has a great advantage in the industrial race. Our country works for the world's market, and we cannot afford

Mills "Skailing," 1882.

the luxury of inefficient labour. Every means should be used to raise the moral tone of the working classes, and this necessity was never greater than at present. Political power is undoubtedly passing into the hands of the masses, and it is a question of the first importance that it should be intelligently and impartially employed.

This supreme necessity of the age was clearly foreseen by

the founders of the thread industry, and particularly by the brothers Peter and Thomas Coats, whose memory Paisley people have good cause to revere. Rarely in history or in fiction can we find two such noble characters; and their

MILLS "SKAILING," 1906.

influence on Paisley has been enormous, and always for good. They have been likened to the Cheerbyle Brothers in *Nicholas Nickleby*, and the comparison is a happy one. But there was a high moral and religious tone about the Brothers Coats which Dickens has not reproduced.

Possessed, at least in their later years, of "wealth beyond the dreams of avarice," money had no corroding influence on their gentle and benevolent natures. The early simplicity of their lives was never changed by the accession of material prosperity. Ostentation and extravagance had no attractions for them. The sole employment which they saw for surplus wealth, was to use it for the elevation of the people among whom their lot was cast. To do their duty faithfully and without display, was their ideal. They

> "Did good by stealth, and blushed to find it fame."

Their wealth had been acquired by honest industry, and they well knew that this was the only sure road to progress. Hence promiscuous alms-giving and misuse of benevolence, were guarded against with vigilant care. They realized that mere wealth showered upon the working classes, would not necessarily conduce to their happiness. They must learn by Christian prudence to make a proper use of the gifts of the Creator. Hence every project for the elevation of the masses in the practice of industry, sobriety, and, above all, in Christian principle, received their liberal and steady support.

Their interest in such societies as the Philosophical Institution was early and steadfast, and ripened into the gifts of the Free Public Library and Museum, and the Observatory. Mr. Thomas Coats' donation to the schools to ensure increased air space and larger playgrounds, was the highest form of charity, dictated by that genial love for the people, which was a controlling motive in his life.

Although from their wealth and influence these brothers might at any time have aspired to high political positions, they felt no call to mingle in such strife. They found their happiness in promoting the welfare of the people among whom they dwelt, and never permitted political or religious differences to influence their actions.

Glasgow Road Promenade, 1906.

Shakspeare says—

"The evil that men do lives after them."

This is true, but there is another saying as true and much older, that

"The path of the just is as the shining light."

The brothers Coats gave a tone to the distribution of wealth, and the sentiments which animated them were equally entertained and acted upon by the other thread manufacturers. They all, without exception, were ever ready to give their personal services as well as pecuniary aid, to every project for the elevation of the people, for the benefit of the feeble and the unfortunate, and for the alleviation of physical suffering. We may cherish the hope that this influence and example will be enduring, and that generations yet to come may have cause to bless and reverence the memory of the wise and liberal men who founded and developed the Thread Industry.

INDEX

	PAGE		PAGE
Abercrombie, T. Graham,	164	Broom, John,	156
Abercrombie, William,	112	Brown, Hugh,	113
Abercorn, Duke of,	161	Brown, William,	9, 179
Abbey Close,	157	Brunton, Dr.,	166, 188
Abbey of Paisley,	159	Burgess, Charles,	112
Aikman,	114	Burns Club,	130
Anchor Thread,	41		
Annie Clark Fund,	105	Caldwell, George,	164
Archibald, George, senr.,	174	Caldwell, James, F.S.A. (Scot.),	8
Archibald, George,	174	Caldwell, "Lady,"	164
Archibald, Robert,	174	Callender, Peter,	144
Arkleston,	114, 153	Canal Bank,	148
Arkwright,	24	Candy-man,	121
Artizans' Institution,	94, 155	Canton crape,	45
Ashburton MSS.,	91	Carriagehill,	152
Ayrshire Fencibles,	44	Carlile, Alexander,	58, 110
		Carlile Family,	56
Balderston, Robert,	9, 106	Carlile, James,	58
Bank of Scotland, old,	112, 138	Carlile, John,	57
Barbour, William, M.P.,	154	Carlile, William, 1703,	57
Bargarran thread,	21	Carlile, William, 1746-1829,	58
Bazaar for Infirmary,	102	Castlehead,	118, 171
Begg, Alexander,	112	Causeyside, old,	110
Bell, Provost R. K.,	143	Central Agency,	62
Berlin Decree,	36	Chadwick, James, & Brother,	63
Black, Colin,	115	Charleston,	151
"Black Peter,"	173, 178	Charleston Drum,	115
Blantyre, Lady,	20	Cheap labour,	32
Bleaching greens,	119	Christie, James E.,	123
Block printers,	153	"Christopher North,"	130, 167
Bobbin wood,	77	Clark, George A.,	40, 97
Boom in Combines,	73	Clark, James, 1747-1829,	35
Brook, Jonas, & Brothers,	63	Clark, James, 1783-1865,	37

	PAGE		PAGE
Clark, James, Chapel House,	9, 38, 97	Dalziel, Robert F.,	112
Clark, James, Ralston,	104	"Daunie Weir."	162
Clark, John, 1791-1864,	37	Death-rate,	185
Clark, John, Gateside,	104, 106	Designers,	148
Clark, J. & J.,	37	Dividends,	73
Clark, Kenneth M.,	105	Drainage,	186
Clark, Patrick,	36	Drill Hall,	168
Clark, Stewart,	43, 105, 106	Dunn Square,	154
Clark Town Halls,	97, 153	Dunn, Sir William, Bart.,	154
Clark, William, -1753,	34	Dundonald, Lord,	161
Clark, William, 1841-1902,	40	Dutch thread,	21
Coats, Andrew,	49	Duffel cloaks,	109
Coats, Archibald,	77, 92		
Coats, Mrs. Archibald,	107	East India Company,	24
Coats, James, 1774-1857,	44	Education Act,	95
Coats, James, 1803-1845,	49	Educational advantages,	188
Coats, Sir James,	51, 90	English Sewing Cotton Company,	63
Coats, James, Junr.,	87, 92, 96, 103, 105		
Coats, J. & P.,	49	Factory system,	193
Coats, J. & P., Limited, Report,	69, 102	Farquharson, Robert,	59
Coats, Sir Peter,	49, 88, 199	Family life,	196
Coats, Peter, Garthland Place,	102	Forbes, James,	112
Coats, Thomas,	49, 86, 92, 94, 155, 199	Forbes Street,	139
Coats, Sir Thomas Glen-,	53	Fountain Gardens,	87
Coats Memorial Church,	99, 168	Fraser, Rev. Wm., D.D.,	92
Cochran, Robert,	91	Free Library and Museum,	88, 168, 185
Coffee Room,	135	Fulton, Humphrey,	45
"Coffin En',"	168		
Colinslee,	114, 152	Gentleman's Magazine,	23, 57
Combination,	62	Gilmour, David,	114, 144, 167
Commercial Hotel,	134	Glen-Coats, Sir Thomas,	83
Contrast of Old and New Paisley,	189	Glenfield, laird of,	114
Corporation of Paisley,	8	Glenfield, the Linn,	153
Cotton,	25	Gleniffer Homes,	147
Craw, William,	113	Gifts of other manufacturers,	193
Crawford, John,	132	Girls' Home,	82
Crompton,	24	Goodlet's "Coffee House,"	162
Crookston Castle,	150	Gordon's Loan,	143
Cross, 1868,	123	Glasgow Road, Sunday promenade,	192
Cross steeple,	127	Grammar School, old,	166, 188

Index

	PAGE		PAGE
Greenlees, John,	113	M'Intyre, William,	114
Guthrie, Robert,	114	MacKean, Provost William,	186
		Mackenzie, Provost Archibald,	187
Half-timers' School,	81, 172	M'Kinlay, Dr. W. B.,	94, 156
Hammills,	161	M'Murchy, James,	114
Hand labour, decay of,	195	MacRobert, Thomas,	156
Hargreaves,	24	Marshall's Lane School,	145
Harper, Archie,	112	Millar, James,	114
Hay, James,	9, 163	Miller, Rev. John,	20
Heddles,	36	Mills "skailing,"	190
Henderson, Rev. A.,	93	Monopoly,	64
High Church steeple,	165	Morgan, John,	112
Holland, machines from,	21	Murray, Provost,	115, 186
Howe, Elias,	32	Museum and Free Library,	88, 168
"Hole in the Wa',"	111, 135		
Holiday trips,	83	Nethercommon,	153
Hope Temple Gardens,	86, 166	Newbery, Mrs. Jessie R.,	8
Hutchison, Archibald,	112	Numbering of thread,	27
		Nurses' Home,	102
Industrial School,	106		
Infirmary,	101, 153	Observatory,	92
Jail Square,	122		
James Clark Bequest Fund,	104	Paisley Magazine,	58
		Paisley Sick Relief Fund,	103
Kerr, Dr. James,	186	Paton, Sir J. Noel,	151
Kerr, Mrs. Gallowhill,	105	Paul, Robert,	39
Kerr, Peter & Son,	59	Pawtucket Mills,	51
Kerr, Robert,	111	Pay, rates of,	75
		Peattie, William,	163
Lamb, James J.,	156	Peesweep Inn,	171
Lang, Howard,	113	"Peter's,"	112, 140
Last canal boat,	179	Pension Fund,	80
Limited Company, formation of,	52	Philips, Provost,	113
Lindsay, James,	156	Philosophical Institution,	88
Lister & Co.,	63	Place of Paisley,	161
		Pollock, Provost,	113
Literary Union,	156, 163	Polson, John,	179
Love, John,	86	Polson, Mrs. John,	134
		Population of Paisley,	182
Macdonald, Hugh,	170	Promenade on Sunday,	192
Macgregor, P. C.,	113		

		PAGE
Protective legislation,	- - -	66
Private benevolences,	- -	108
Privations,	- - -	116
Prize Essay,	- - -	94
Ragged School,	- - -	112
Religion in school,	- - -	145
Risk, Thomas,	- - -	112
Robertson, J. & J.,	- - -	112
Robertson, John,	- - -	91
Rob Roy Close,	- - -	162
Ross & Duncan,	- - -	46
Rowat, Robert.	- - -	113
Rowbank water scheme,	- -	186
Royal Alexandra Infirmary,	-	101, 153
Royal Victoria Eye Infirmary,	-	187
Russell, Robert,	- - -	163
Rye water scheme,	- - -	186
Saracen's Head Inn,	- - -	128
Scott, Matthew,	- - -	112
Seedhills Bridge,	- - -	161
Seedhills Mills,	- - -	39
Sempill's House,	- - -	162
Sewing machine,	- - -	32
Shaw, Christian,	- - -	19, 174
Shaw, John, Bargarran,	- -	19
Shaw, John,	- - -	156
Shaw, Willie,	- - -	122
Shawl Exhibition,	- - -	91
Shawl trade, decay of,	- -	30
Singer Co.,	- - -	32
Small, William,	- - -	86
Smith, Alexander,	- - -	151
Smith, R. A.,	- - -	44
Speirs, David,	- - -	112
Spinning-wheel,	- - -	17
Spools,	- - -	28, 38, 77
Stanley Castle,	- - -	170

		PAGE
Strikes,	- - - - -	84
Sunday night at Gibb's,	- -	135
Symington, J. M.,	- - -	113
Tannahill Concert,	- - -	101, 153
Tannahill's Hole,	- - -	173
Tannahill, Robert,	-	44, 153, 169, 172
Tearers,	- - - - -	153
Technical College,	- - -	96
"Teuch Geordie,"	- - -	121, 168
Teetotal Tower,	- - -	164
Thread girls,	- - - -	190
Thread numbering,	- - -	27
Thread manufacturers, list of,	-	59
Tolbooth,	- - - -	126
Town's House stair,	- - -	131
United States,	- - - -	26, 49
Valuation of Paisley,	- -	184
Walker,	- - - - -	112
Walker, Drybrough & Co.,	-	114
Water supply,	- - - -	185
Water Wynd,	- - - -	137
"Watty and Meg,"	- - -	162
Watson, Richard,	- - -	115
Western Bank,	- - -	112
"Wee Well,"	- - - -	170
Whitehill,	- - - -	112
Wheeler & Wilson,	- - -	32
Whyte, James,	- - - -	45
Wilson, Alexander,	- - -	36
Wilson, Professor John,	-	130, 167
Wilson, Provost David,	- -	185
Witches,	- - - -	19, 173
Young Men's Christian Association,	-	164
Yuill, John,	- - - - -	112

BY THE SAME AUTHOR

WITH 10 FACSIMILE REPRODUCTIONS IN COLOURS OF PAISLEY SHAWLS
and Numerous other Illustrations, including Portraits of the leading
Manufacturers and Public Men of the Time.
Crown Quarto. Art Linen Binding. Gilt Top. Price 7s. 6d. nett.

THE PAISLEY SHAWL
AND THE MEN WHO PRODUCED IT

PRESS NOTICES.

"An interesting and very beautifully illustrated memorial of a now closed chapter in the history of British manufacture."—*Times*.

"'The Epoch of the Shawl Trade in Paisley,' writes the author of this interesting volume, 'is now rounded off. Like a flower it came up, blossomed, and decayed.' Even thus, in Paisley, does the poetic imagination weave garlands of blooming thoughts round textile fabrics. The book, however, is description and history, not an effusion of creative art. The shawls are now rarities sought for by collectors. To such persons this volume must prove uncommonly valuable as explaining, both by pictures and by written descriptions, the technical excellences of garments that must always rank among the most wonderful productions of the world-old craft of the weaver."—*Scotsman*.

"Mr. Blair is one of the few who still possess the necessary qualifications for writing a record of the lost trade, for he was brought up in it. He has performed his task with the competence of a craftsman and with the enthusiasm of a man who looks back on scenes to which distance and intervening success combine to lend enchantment. His treatment is singularly vivid and interesting, even when the picture appears somewhat more highly coloured than is quite consistent with absolute truth to nature. The illustrations consist mainly of shawl patterns, reproduced in colour. Their execution is admirable, and the striking effect which they produce might almost be expected to bring our grandmothers' favourite Paisley shawls into fashion again."—*Glasgow Herald*.

"Mr. Matthew Blair, who is Chairman of the Incorporated Weaving, Dyeing, and Printing College of Glasgow, has been well advised in writing a short history of what he rightly terms an illustrious period in the history of his native town. . . . Mr. Blair, whose treatment of his subject proves that he has inherited no small share of the literary skill of the race of weaver poets, has taken pains to point out how the educational influence of this highly technical toil produced the old class of cultured and ingenious weavers. By so doing he has made his handsome monograph on the Paisley shawl not only a valuable record of a bygone industry, but one which, far from being dull to the general reader, demonstrates very prettily that nothing human need be alien to us. The book is beautifully illustrated by plates representing the old weavers and their work."—*Athenaum*.

PAISLEY: ALEXANDER GARDNER,
Publisher by Appointment to the late Queen Victoria

CPSIA information can be obtained
at www.ICGtesting.com
Printed in the USA
BVHW04*1436250918
528446BV00011B/97/P